D0742073

THE GRAY MARE'S COLTS

GOLDEN GATE JUNIOR BOOKS
San Carlos · California

THE
GRAY MARE'S COLTS

JUDY VAN DER VEER

drawings by
Bernard Garbutt

A WORLD FAMOUS HORSE STORY Selection

Copyright © 1971 by Judy Van der Veer
All rights reserved
ISBNs: Trade 0-87464-172-1 Library 0-87464-173-X
Library of Congress catalog card number 79-157855
Lithographed in the United States of America
by Anderson, Ritchie & Simon, Los Angeles

To the memory of Alex
who had more understanding of horses
and more music in his heart
than anyone we have ever known

CONTENTS

THE GRAY MARE'S COLTS

THE GRAY MARE

I have a son of hers, and a daughter, and two of her grand-children. So far as I know, these are the only living descendants of the old gray mare. But, in a certain way, all my horses are the children of the gray mare, for she was the beginning of the horses in my life. There are direct causes and indirect causes of the happenings on this earth. The gray mare was the cause of Pepper, Pericles and Win-kie, Ramona and Don Ramon, and the indirect cause of all the other horses that live here on this ranch. The whole pattern of my life was changed when I became owner of the gray mare in the days when she and I were young.

Always that was what I wanted—horses. She was my first, and I kept her until she grew old, and her heart stopped beating one day when she lay down on the sun-warmed earth. The older she grew, the more wonderful she became. When we were young we didn't know each other so well. I was strange to the ways of horses, but of course I thought I knew everything. If I knew half as much now as I thought I knew then, if I were half as good a rider now as I thought I was then, I would truly be the world's leading authority on horses and riding. The way it is now, the more I learn about horses the more I realize that there is more and more to be learned.

The poor gray mare—when she was young! I do not like to remember all she had to put up with from me. And she, in those days, had little patience with me, and no affection at all. Time mellowed us both. Before she died she had acquired patience and some affection and developed more and more lovable qualities. Or perhaps those qualities had been there all along and I had just begun to see them.

Toward the end she became absent-minded and perhaps a little hard of hearing, and maybe she didn't see too well. If one of us went near her while she was grazing, she didn't even notice us at first, then suddenly did, and was startled. To cover up her confusion she'd chatter at us, nickering excitedly as if to say mercy me and oh my goodness, child, I didn't see you at first, well isn't this nice. . . .

All the other horses thought she was wonderful, always. Even when she was in her dotage the geldings fell in love with her each spring and imagined themselves to be young stallions. She was the leader of the herd, and wherever she went they followed.

I wanted her to live as long as possible and be as happy as possible, to make up for all the hardships I had caused her when I was a child. So, as her health began to fail, it was no novelty to put in an emergency call for the vet at any hour of the day or night. I think perhaps he was relieved when at last she lay down and died.

She was beginning to be old when she gave birth to Pepper, and was very old when she had her last foal, Winkie. Between them came the gray colt, Pericles, who grew old but stayed fat and lively, especially in the spring. Winkie, black and shining, has had one daughter and one son. Pepper is dead.

These three the old gray mare foaled. But all the others are, in a way, hers too, for it is because of her that they are here.

And it is because of her that other horses have come into my life. Mohammed said, "Happiness is in the feet of horses . . . even unto the end of the world." It was the hoofs of the gray mare that took me on trails I would never have found without her, that led me to ranch country and my home in the hills.

When first I met her I was a city child in Southern California. San Diego was not then so big as it is now, and there were canyons and vacant lots everywhere. One day I saw a neighbor girl riding her beautiful white mare. If she could have a horse in the city, why couldn't I? It took a great deal of emoting and pestering of parents, but finally I had my way.

The neighbor girl and I rode together. It was an hour's ride to get us outside the city. We took devious ways, through alleys, finding which streets were innocent of pavement. Once free of the city, we could smell the wonderful fragrance of the sage, artemesia and all else that grows on the hills.

This is part of the delicious smell of horses. The ranch where my horses and I now live has canyons, hills and meadows filled with that fragrance. It is a scent that clings to the coats of all the horses I have loved.

THE MESA

Where now city and cement cover the earth there was once a beautiful wild mesa. Winter rains covered it with grass, spring covered it with flowers. There was also an old neglected olive orchard, and after enough rain fell there was a pond.

When I was about seventeen I spent every day there and the gray mare spent every other day. On alternate days my companion was Johnny, a strawberry roan with a white blaze on his face and flashy white socks. Every day my companion was an airedale named Mike.

The valley below was given over to dairy ranches. After rains greened the mesa it was my job to drive a herd of dairy cows to graze up there. For this service I was paid seven dollars a week and given my midday meal. It seemed a large amount of money to me. It paid for my horses' hay, and when I saved carefully I had money left over with which to buy a pretty dress now and again. Though I liked wearing jeans and being with horses and cows, I also liked going to dances with the ranch boys in the old valley schoolhouse.

My parents were not pleased with this life I had elected to lead. They regretted that they ever let me have the gray mare in the first place. She was the cause of all their trouble with me. If I hadn't taken to riding off on her, I might have finished high school, perhaps even gone to college. Her hoofs were taking me far from any life my family could plan for me.

But my mother was willing to waken me before daylight every morning, serve me breakfast, and wistfully wave good-by as I and my dog and horse hurried away. We clattered along city streets, followed a canyon down into a valley, crossed the valley to the dairy. Then the cows were let out of the corral, the big roaring bull released from his pen. The cows climbed eagerly up the trail to the mesa, thinking of all the grass they could enjoy.

There were meadow larks on the mesa and redwing blackbirds singing in the valley. Even now when I hear meadow larks and blackbirds I think of that mesa and the days I spent there. I watched rabbits and squirrels which Mike chased. I drove the cows to the best patch of grass I could find and kept them from straying far all the morning. Once they settled down to grazing, I could unbridle my horse. Curiously, perhaps, the sound of a grazing horse has become mixed in my mind with the enjoyment of reading.

In those days there were paperback books called "Little Blue Books." Two or three of them could fit into my pocket. They cost five cents apiece and they contained the best literature. I read the stories of the operas, I read poetry and philosophy. I read classic fiction and great essays. I, who had refused to go to school any longer, was receiving an education.

I've thought many times since that I have the gray mare to thank for my book learning as well as for other things. Had I not had her hoofs to carry me I would not have had the dairy job. I wouldn't have known anything about horses, mesas, cows—or literature. I wouldn't have even had Johnny who was an extra-good horse.

Somehow, by saving, scrimping, arguing with my family, I had managed to buy Johnny at a bargain price. My parents certainly put up with a lot!

Johnny was five years old then and so pretty and lively that my heart overflowed with pride whenever I looked at him. Soon I discovered why he had been sold so cheap. Johnny was what is called stable-bound. He didn't want to leave home. Before I had ridden him five minutes away from his barn he would rear, spin around, and head for home. When I argued with him he bucked me off.

Otherwise, he was charming. He loved being with a human, enjoyed petting and conversation. I taught him to shake hands, paw to count how old he was, to kneel down. But for a long while I couldn't make him go anywhere without a ferocious disagreement.

One day I thought of an idea that might possibly work. Instead of getting on him at once, I walked by his left side, holding the reins as if I were riding. I turned him to the right and left as I walked beside him, circled him, walked him in figure eights, talked to him constantly. This time he didn't try to whirl and race for home. After I trudged beside him for half a mile, I put a foot in the stirrup as he moved forward. I rode along standing up for a few minutes before I swung my right leg over the saddle. I kept talking and he kept walking.

I lifted him into a gallop and he swung along as if he'd forgotten all about going home. For days after that, whenever I started for a ride, I walked beside Johnny first and we had no more problems.

He was one who loved excitement and to be in a parade made him prance. He liked to rear and show off, but when he did this he did it so lightly that I had no trouble staying on him.

Both Johnny and the gray mare soon learned about driving cattle anywhere and needed no guidance from my hand on the reins. Each of them would turn to shoo a laggard cow along, and Johnny reached out to bite rumps of slow ones.

Occasionally we saw a big herd of beef cattle being driven down the mesa road to the stockyards in the city. When this happened the dairy cows were thrilled and wanted to join the herd. I couldn't blame them for they had little excitement in their lives and the red, white-faced cattle were pretty and wild-looking. The big dairy bull, of course, was all for mingling at once. He bellowed and pawed the grass and started after the cattle. I was glad that my horse could run fast and turn quickly or we would never have got him back.

I felt sorry for the cattle that were going to slaughter, but I couldn't help but admire the cowboys. I loved cowboys almost as much as I loved horses.

At noon I drove the cows to the pond, waited for all of them to drink, then drove them to the old olive orchard for a siesta in the shade. After they settled to chew cuds, I hurried down to the ranch house, unsaddled and fed my horse hay and went in for the noon meal. It was always the same, fried mutton chops. Everybody ate mutton because the hired man had heard that mutton was good for his arteries which he feared were hardening. I suppose that mutton was the worst thing he could have eaten, but it seemed to do him no harm. As for me, I was so hungry from being outdoors that any food was great.

After we had eaten, I saddled and rode back to the cows. They had to be made to get up and start grazing again, else they'd slumber all afternoon and not eat enough grass to produce the quantities of milk demanded of them. They moaned and groaned as they got up, awkwardly, hind end first, as cows do, but once I took them to a grassy spot they went at it cheerfully.

When it rained my horse and I found shelter in a little draw where a big protective boulder sloped over the bank. It didn't bother us to get wet. I read the story of the opera "Carmen" one rainy afternoon as I huddled there, and it was beautiful. But the best to read in the rain was anything by Thomas Hardy. And "Wuthering Heights" was wonderful to read with rain, like tears, on the pages.

Sometimes one of the ranch boys from the valley would

ride up to the mesa to sit and talk for awhile. Once a hand-some young motorcycle cop rode off the highway and came bumping over the uneven terrain.

At the sight and sound of his machine, the gray mare went frantic and nearly pulled up the bush to which she was tied. I hurried to try to soothe her, and, at the same time the cows, as frightened as she, stampeded. I had to jump on my excited mare and ride fast to circle the cows and get them headed toward a draw where there was grass and from which they couldn't see the loud mon-ster. By the time I got them settled and had ridden back, the young man was unhappy.

He was apologetic about the confusion he had caused and he was dismayed at a flat tire on his motorcycle. He had ridden over one of the cacti family, a small dome-like thing with hard sharp spikes. We had little conver-sation as he spent his time cussing and putting on a tire patch. When this was accomplished, he rode out of my life forever.

For the most part, however, I had only dog, horse and cows for companions and I liked talking to them. I liked the cows, and learned that each was a distinct indi-vidual. This was, perhaps, a strange way for a teen-age girl to spend her days, but they were good days to me.

Mid-afternoon was the time to take the cows back to the dairy. Soon it would be milking time. Each cow knew her own stanchion in the barn and the bull knew that now it was time for him to go into his high-fenced pen. At the thought of this he began to grumble, to roar and paw the ground. When the gray mare and I couldn't make him go in, the hired man took after him with a pitchfork. That brought results, though after the gate was shut the bull always continued to complain.

But tomorrow he could go out again and so could we all. Each evening I headed back to the city and a different —and hated—way of life.

At last my parents grew so annoyed at my daily absences that they decided to make a change. They had finally concluded that the only way to keep me at home was to buy a place in the country.

The day we moved was the happiest day of my life. I rode the gray mare and led Johnny, and every hoofbeat put the city further behind us.

MAIRZIE

One time a neighbor, Tex, wanted to buy a cow from me and said he'd trade a little chestnut mare as part-payment. I said yes, before I'd given it any thought, but afterwards I didn't think I wanted the mare as she was old and not much good, though she was very pretty. She'd led a hard life, having been a rent stable horse. She was bitter and hated the whole world.

I wished I'd thought it over more before I'd told Tex I'd take her; then, though I tried to back out, I couldn't. Tex simply turned the mare loose, and when irate neighbors complained, he said she was mine and I said she was his. It went on like that for quite awhile, until the neighbors threatened to shoot the mare. Even then, if it hadn't been for Red, I'd probably still have been trying to avoid ownership.

Red and his young wife and two small children had moved to a ranch next to mine. That is, if you could call it a ranch. There was a shack of a house on some unkempt acres, but it was a million times better than living in town and Red appreciated it. He had had little experience with cows and horses, but right away he knew that cows and horses were exactly what he liked and wanted. He took an interest in the old mare, whom we named Mairzie (from the song, "Mairzie Doats"), and one day he caught her and jumped on her bareback. From her withers forward Mairzie stood motionless, but she kicked her hind legs up and down, believing that she was bucking fiercely. Red, who at that time knew little about sticking on a horse, had no difficulty riding her stiff up-and-down motion, just like being on a see-saw. It was the funniest exhibition of bucking we'd ever seen, and the more we laughed at her, the further old Mairzie pinned back her ears.

She hated us. She hated all people and all other horses and all cows and dogs. Ready to bite us, she'd get a mean, pinched-up look about her nostrils when we went near her. If we jumped on her bareback we had to learn to jump in a hurry, for she'd reach around and bite our rears before we could swing on.

Her attitude toward any horse being ridden while she was free in pasture was that the horse was a sucker, and this thought made her so furious that she'd chase any horse that was being ridden past her. She was too old and stiff to run very fast, but she looked like a demon with her ears flat back and her long teeth bared. It was fun to let unsuspecting strangers ride into the pasture, then watch them ride for their lives when Mairzie went charging after them. No amount of yelling or arm-waving would drive her back. The only thing to do was to fill your pockets with stones to throw at her. Even if your aim, like mine, was poor, she respected a thrown stone.

One day Red, who kept Mairzie at his place most of the time, came riding along on her. "Look," said he, "I've just taught old Mairzie something." And he picked up his reins and put her into a lovely running walk.

I had to explain, "You didn't teach her anything, she's taught you. She's just taught you how to use your hands and collect a horse." Red saw the truth of this, and, since he had the right attitude, very quickly became an excellent rider. He always gave Mairzie credit for teaching him how to ride.

And Mairzie taught Red's little daughter how to ride too. Bonnie was only six years old and had never been around horses before, but she adored Mairzie. Mairzie, who enjoyed kicking and biting Red and me, never even put back her ears at Bonnie. Bonnie would brush Mairzie's coat until it was soft and glossy and Mairzie would look very pleased.

Only one other thing ever made her look so pleased. That was when she'd try, in her feeble way, to buck Red off, and Red would oblige by calling out in a frightened voice, "Oh Mairzie!" And deliberately fall off her. He said nothing else made Mairzie so happy and, after the hard life she had led, she deserved all the happiness she could have. Red really was a good guy.

Spring came and we wondered if a colt would sweeten Mairzie's soul, or only make her more fierce, in a protective sort of way. She had the look of a really well-bred animal and we knew she'd have a beautiful colt. One day when the air was sweet with wild lilac and the sky was deep blue between moving white clouds and the wind blew the wild grasses in little running waves, we took Mairzie to Pedro's meadow. Pedro was a chestnut stallion with a flaxen mane and tail, very well built, handsome enough to be a good match for Mairzie.

It was as if Mairzie knew where she was going—she danced all the way. When we turned her free in the meadow she ran over the green grass like a colt, and Pedro, shouting, came running with long strides to meet her. Then Mairzie, turning coy, knowing the fun of courtship, fled, and Pedro, running faster, circled around her and pranced to show off his beauty and reared straight up in the air. The meadow lay like a cupped hand and the colored hills rose up and the sky, with its white clouds, seemed in motion to match the motion in the meadow.

Mairzie was so quiet and contented after the mating that we were sure she was in foal. It was a disappointment later to discover that she was not.

We sent her to stay for two months with Beau Bud, a palomino who belonged to our friend Rusty and one of the best-mannered stallions I've ever known. Rusty was a whiz at training stallions. A group of us rode together a great deal that summer and Rusty let me ride Bud one moonlight night. That ride turned out to be one I like to keep remembering. Bud's thick white mane looked so very white in the moonlight and his neck so very gold. But the joy of him was the way he stepped, as if springs were concealed in his little hoofs. I never rode a better horse and we kept hoping old Mairzie would have a foal by him.

But she didn't. By then my stallion, Don Roscoe, was old enough to be a father, but he had no better luck with her than the others.

Anyway, it didn't really matter. Mairzie had enjoyed her romances and she was having a good home in her old age, which she deserved after all that she had been through. She had to work a little when Red's car broke down and he used Mairzie as transportation to his job. She would be walking quietly along on the way to work and then she'd think maybe Red wasn't noticing her very closely. So, carefully, she'd try to turn around. She'd turn in a half-circle, hoping Red wouldn't catch on. She didn't give him any argument when he turned her back, just sighed because her plan hadn't worked, then trudged on, waiting for the time when he'd relax so she could try again.

When Red's car was finally repaired she was retired once more, turned out in the hills with the others. Geldings always love old mares and mine followed Mairzie devotedly, though she made it clear that she thought them all silly fools. She bit and kicked them but they adored her anyway.

She was useful, for she brought the whole herd home for me to see every morning. Old horses have a hard time staying fat and, as pasture grass became sparse, the way it does toward fall, I started giving Mairzie a pan of grain every morning. So of course she came down the hill for her breakfast and all the others tagged along. But she didn't wait patiently by the gate. It was an ordinary wire gate, with a loop of wire at the top and the bottom of the gate post, and Mairzie's clever nose pushed the loops up and down. Then, while the other horses she had released ran happily out on the road, Mairzie hammered on the barn door with one front hoof, cross at me for being so slow to feed her.

When we wired the gate so that she couldn't open it, she was enraged and she pawed until she was lost in a dust cloud. As soon as I had let her through, she would rush to the barn, sometimes to kick the side of it by way of self-expression. And all the time she was eating she was stamping, kicking and biting at the chickens that came pecking around. Quite frequently the side of the barn would receive another wallop just for good measure.

Of all the horses I've met, Mairzie is one that I am exceedingly glad to have known. It made us feel good to know that at least one weary old mare had a long rest and enough to eat before she died.

PENNY
AND PERICLES

I named him Halfpenny because everyone said that he wasn't worth a cent. Naturally, his name dwindled to Penny. By the time I owned him he was nearly half a year old.

I had often seen him and his mother near a shack where the old man who owned them lived. Though he was not the most beautiful of colts, he was endearing as all colts are. His mother was a good sorrel mare. The colt was also red, with a neat white stripe down his face. He was not finely built, his bones were big. His face was not pretty because he had somewhat of a Roman nose. The old man said that he was part Hambletonian. Hambletonians are good horses.

On a certain day one fall, I rode by the old man's shack and didn't see mare or colt. A dozen dogs of mixed varieties came to bark at me as I rode in to inquire about the mare and colt. I noted that the old man's mule was there, acting lonesome and hee-hawing. The old man had a few head of cattle with never enough pasture for them. He owned many dogs, all of which he loved, and he seemingly enjoyed the mare and colt. He was a kind old man.

I remembered a morning when I'd been riding toward his shack and had watched the old man on his mule bring home a bull which obviously had strayed and did not want to come home. The bull was bellowing, snorting, pawing the earth, and getting down on his knees before the mule and his rider. The old man kept urging the mule toward the bull and the bull kept bellowing, snorting, pawing the earth, dropping to his knees—and backing in the direction man and mule wanted him to go. Neither the mule nor the old man seemed to be in the least dismayed. Soon they had the bull safely in his corral. I was impressed.

This day, as I rode toward the shack, the old man came out to yell at the dogs not to bite my horse. They obeyed him at once.

"Where's the mare and colt?" I asked.

The old man looked sad. "I didn't have enough pasture for them. Nor no money to buy them feed. So I sold them. I had to go sell them to the zoo in the city."

"The zoo?"

"Well, better for them to be killed and fed to the lions than to starve. Don't you think? Mebbe not. I don't know. I feel awful bad."

"When did you take them?"

"This mornin'. Had an awful time loadin' them into my truck. I feel just awful."

"Oh," I said rashly, "I'd have bought them. Can you go and get them back?"

"I'll try." And the old man started hurrying toward his rickety truck.

I didn't know what to expect and rode home feeling sorrowful. Also, I was worried. I didn't have much money and here I was, proposing to buy, then feed two animals I really had no business to own.

Before dark the old man's truck came rattling to my barn. In it was only the sorrel colt. He was plunging about, completely terrified.

"They already went and kilt the mare," the old man explained, and began unloading the colt whose hoofs were flying in all directions at once. The colt had never been halter-broken or taught to lead and it took a deal of pushing and pulling to get him into a stall. We had to keep dodging hoofs.

He stood quivering and rolling his eyes at us. His eyes were wild. He began whinnying, no doubt longing for the comfort his mother could provide. I hurried to give him hay, grain and a bucket of water.

"He'll make a dandy horse for you someday," the old man prophesied. "I give them back their money for him. All you owe me is five dollars."

That didn't seem to be too bad a deal.

After the old man left I went into the stall and began talking softly to the colt. My voice seemed to soothe him, though he wouldn't trust me to put a hand on him. Soon he ate his grain, then he started to enjoy his hay.

He was thin. He wouldn't have provided much of a meal for any zoo animal. If he were fed well I could see no reason why he shouldn't grow to normal size, even though he might have done better with his mother's milk to help. However, since the mare had been hungry, probably she hadn't produced much milk.

The colt was so lonely that even though he was afraid of me, he whinnied when I left.

I was with him early the next morning, offering food and friendship. The food he accepted. He continued to roll wild eyes at me and shy away from an outstretched hand. I could understand. He longed for his own pasture, even if it was a poor one. It was the only place he had ever known. He was accustomed to the cows, the mule, the old man and the dogs. Most of all, the mare who was his mother meant safety and comfort. Then suddenly had come the trip to the zoo in the city. He had been terrified. At the zoo he had heard horrifying sounds, smelled frightening things. Worst of all, his mother had been taken away. Then he had had another journey in the truck and had ended up in an unfamiliar place where the only good thing was that he had enough to eat and drink. But he could not seem to escape from this strange human who frightened him, even though the human made soft noises at him.

After a week, his attitude was unchanged. It was time for me to be forceful about my intentions. I cornered him, held him tight, slipped a halter, with lead rope attached, on him. He shivered and shook and his eyes kept rolling.

He struck out with front hoofs. While he could not escape I rubbed him with my hands, said soft words, brushed him. Gradually he relaxed. He began to like this.

For the next few days the same thing happened to him. Finally, my ministrations neither surprised nor startled. Then it was time carefully to teach him how to lead. Around the stall we went, I pulling him to the side and slightly off balance when he would not come. At last, at the tug of the lead rope he stepped forward to put a quivering, nervous nose into my cupped hand.

I felt that he wanted to trust me, but that he had to conquer his own fears first. I was careful not to press myself upon him for very long at a time. A short lesson every day was best. By now I was calling him Penny.

After awhile Penny led so well that I took him out into the corral and walked him around. From there he saw the other horses and he whinnied at them. They stared at him with interest.

The gray mare's second son, Pericles, came to the gate. I let him into the corral. It would do Penny good to know someone who was near his own age.

The eyes of both young horses bulged, nostrils widened, ears were interestedly rigid. Noses poked forward. The gray mare came to the fence to shout at her son to be careful, a strange colt might be dangerous. Pericles was too fascinated with Penny to pay any attention to her. Penny, lonely for others of his kind, was delighted to see Pericles.

The colts nosed each other and squealed. They struck out with front hoofs, whirled to pretend to kick. Then they were nuzzling each other and nipping gently. From that time on they were firm friends.

Because of Pericles to introduce Penny to others, I was able to turn him out in pasture sooner than I had planned. By that time the older horses had grown used to seeing him—in the corral, anyway. He and Pericles raced and played together, nuzzled each other, grazed nose to nose.

Like many a gray, Pericles had been born black. Later, he turned the color of steel-dust. In his old age he was as gray as his mother.

In those days I was completely stupid about training horses. I started riding my colts too young. It is better to wait until a colt is three or even four years old before riding him. But back then, I would look at a colt of about two and a half and couldn't wait to get on him. A colt ridden too much when he is too young is likely to grow into a lazy horse.

Pericles presented few problems. A colt will buck if he is startled, or if he feels overly playful, or if he has intent to get "this thing" off his back. I was careful not to startle Pericles, or to let him get away with feeling too frisky. He was so amazed at the whole procedure that he didn't even think about bucking off a rider. He was surprised at weight on his back and felt that he had to move carefully. It is only after some experience of carrying a rider that my colts ever feel capable of bucking and rebelling.

The very first time I tried out Pericles, he went so well that I rode him into town to pick up the mail. The distance was three miles one way, but I knew I could take trails through a dry riverbed where the landing would be on soft sand in case he decided to remove me. I rode him a little every day, teaching him about reining, teaching him to do a fast little running walk.

Pericles learned willingly and we had no trouble at all until the day we met—of all things—a peacock.

Pericles could not believe that such a creature really existed and stopped to stare at it in horror. The peacock suddenly spread out his beautiful tail and Pericles turned and bolted toward home. I managed to slow him down, then stopped and turned him before he had hurried half a mile.

Pericles should not have been so frightened for the reason that he wasn't being ridden alone. My friend Myrtle was traveling with us on her mare, Babe, and Babe was brave about the peacock. Usually a horse is not so terrified at an unusual sight if he is with another horse who is not afraid.

Myrtle, much amused, sat on Babe and waited for our return. Pericles' eyes were bulging and he was snorting as we came back in sight of Myrtle, her horse and the peacock. Then, immediately, he whirled and was sure that home was the only safe place. Again I turned him and urged him forward. He reared, and as he came down he plunged forward to land on four of the stiffest legs I'd ever felt under me. That landing jarred my backbone and all my teeth.

Before I had recovered, he whirled once more toward home. Again I turned him, urged him—and up he went, to lunge and then to land with the same crashing jar.

This performance Pericles repeated many times before the peacock, not interested, walked away and disappeared. On reflection, I think I would have been wiser to have dismounted and led Pericles past this threat.

The peacock incident taught Pericles something which he considered of great advantage to himself. Whenever he saw anything which displeased him, he used the same tactic. He grew expert at rearing high, lunging forward as he descended, and offering something like a crash landing to his rider.

Only time and determined efforts on my part cured him. He became a fine horse, and only one thing disturbed him very much. This was the sight of a rattlesnake.

When summer days were hot, Pericles never felt lively. Heat bothered him more than it does most horses. If I were riding him out to bring in the cows and saw a rattlesnake, I would immediately turn and race him toward home. I wanted to grab a long-handled hoe with which I could dispatch the snake more quickly than if I were to throw rocks at him. With hoe held high, I would turn and race Pericles back to the rattlesnake.

When we are on a trail far from home and animals we never bother any rattlesnakes we see. After all, the earth is as much theirs as it is ours. Why should we kill a snake that has no desire to harm us? But Pericles thought differently. He would shy, whirl and snort at anything that looked even remotely like a snake. I reasoned that his reaction was because the sight of a snake made him do what he most wanted not to do—run on a hot day.

The first time I tried to ride Penny he didn't like it,

even before I was on his back. I had the impression that a colt should be mounted slowly, should not be startled. Put a foot in the stirrup carefully, slowly edge into the saddle. Before I got there I was on the ground. Penny ran bucking away, turned to stare and snort, then walked back as if to wonder what I was doing down there.

I tried again and found myself hitting the ground with even more speed and force. Again Penny returned to peer down at me with wonderment.

By the fourth try I was beginning to realize I was going at this the wrong way. So I flung myself into the saddle as quickly as I could. Penny just stood there, not in the least amazed. I urged him forward and he walked along like a well-trained horse.

The spring that he was five years old Penny suddenly became extremely lively, and all that spring and summer he wanted to go everywhere at top speed. He was so light on his feet and so delightful to ride that I invited Myrtle to come and ride him for a day while I rode with her on Pericles. She and Penny had a grand time. We rode far back into the hills where the wild lilac was like a blue cloud on the slopes and the air was drenched with sweetness. We saw three deer, one coyote and a small red fox.

My horses are always entranced by the sight of deer, and the only time Penny ever willingly stood still was to stare at these beautiful animals. The rest of the time he seemed to be floating along on hoofs as light as clouds.

All that summer he was eager to travel. When fall came he lost that excess energy and never afterwards regained it. He remained a good horse, willing to go anywhere, any time, but that strange lifting of the spirits was gone. We never knew why it happened or why it stopped happening.

A few years later, Penny's right eye became troublesome, weeping, with a thickness seeming to grow across it. Medication didn't help. We trailered him to the large animal hospital and there his eye had to be removed because the trouble was cancer. The vet did a neat job and sewed the lid shut so that there would be no gaping red hole where the eye used to be. It was some days before Penny came home.

Pericles missed his friend, whinnied and looked for him. When Penny was unloaded from the trailer and turned into his pasture Pericles came rushing to nose him. Each horse touched the other softly, nickered and began to play. But Penny felt awkward, being able to see only to the left.

In order to see both ways, Penny had to learn to swing his head around. In time he grew used to this, but there were scratches on the right side of his face when he was in the hill pasture and went through brush.

Animals do not think or reason in the same way that people do, so I do not know how Pericles sensed or knew that Penny needed help. But somehow he did. We began to notice that when the horses were out in rough terrain Pericles kept himself close to Penny's blind side. He became a seeing-eye horse to guide Penny over rocks, through thick chapparal. I think that, with the help of his friend, Penny would have done all right even if he had been blind in both eyes.

CHERIE

When first I saw her she was small, thin and sick, standing in a stall with her mother who looked nearly ready to die. The little foal had tearful eyes and a running nose, she was like some forlorn child with a bad cold. I looked into her eyes, beyond the tears, and they had golden flecks in them like the hazel eyes of her sire's. I had met him once and admired him. He was a buckskin, with strange, almost golden eyes. He was said to be mostly Arabian, and he looked it.

I turned to the boy Bill who owned mare and foal. "But they are so sick."

"I know. I'm doing everything I can. I've had the vet. The old mare seems to have pneumonia."

Later, after I'd returned home from Bill's place, I kept thinking about the little filly. I had never seen a foal look so sad. Her coat did not lie smoothly as does the coat of a healthy foal. It was a buckskin color, but darker than her sire's coat. Her legs, mane and tail were black. She wore a white star between her weeping eyes.

A few days later I saw Bill again. "The old mare died. Can you take care of the foal? I haven't a cow, and she'll need bottles of milk."

So the little filly came riding to me, propped between the back and front seats of an old sedan. We unloaded her and she made a strange squawking sound.

"She's hoarse," Bill explained. "She's whinnied so much for her mother that she's lost her voice."

It was a warm spring day so we didn't put the filly in the barn. Bill had already taught her to lead and we led her into the fenced yard around the house. It was a good safe place for her. I went into the kitchen to heat up some milk while Bill stood petting her. She continued to make her odd little hoarse sounds. Her eyes were still tearful and her nose stuffy, but it seemed to me she was a little better.

I added some water and some sweet syrup to the warm milk. I knew that a mare's milk is sweeter than a cow's. I filled a bottle, put a rubber nipple on it, offered it to the foal. "Her name is Cherie," the boy said. "Here, Cherie, have some."

Cherie would not. Hungry as she was, she didn't like the rubbery smell. She turned her head and squawked for her real mother.

I said, "We'll have to force her to taste it. Once she gets a taste she's sure to drink."

Bill held her, I forced the nipple into her mouth, she tasted the sweet warm milk. Then she sucked it up very fast and wanted more. I let her have one more bottleful. I didn't want her to drink too much at once. She followed us around and squawked like a little chicken.

Foals nurse often and don't drink much at one time. I had to feed Cherie about once an hour. I was glad that she was no younger. It is difficult to raise a new foal on a bottle. Calves are easy to raise because their mothers give them all the anti-biotics they need before they are born. A foal must receive necessary aids from its mother's milk.

Later, when Cherie was old enough to be on solid food, I provided pellets for her, pellets which are used for feeding calves and contain all good vitamins and minerals. We kept a panful of them in the yard where she could eat whenever she liked. Also, she needed much more milk and this she had. She learned to come to the kitchen door and squawk for it if ever I was slow to serve her.

I had thought that once she became well fed she would cease to feel lonely for her mother, but she did not. She needed the nuzzling, the warm touching a mare provides for her young.

This I gave her as best I could. I hugged her and petted her. I brushed her coat and her mane and tail. When she settled down to sleep on sun-warmed grass I would lie down close beside her. None of this was any hardship for me.

As she recovered from her cold, she grew playful and it was her delight to run races with people, since she had no colt to play with. My young niece, Mary, came for a vacation and she and Cherie spent hours together.

I kept feeding Cherie bottles of milk, long past the age when most colts are weaned. I didn't want her to have the look of an underprivileged colt or calf. This happens to these little ones when they are weaned too young. They look thin in most places, but they have huge, sagging bellies. I wanted Cherie to grow to be a beautiful mare, and she did. Until she was middle-aged and had her first colt, she continued to think that I was her mother. If I rode her to town for the mail, I had to buy her a bottle of pop, which she enjoyed as much as she enjoyed her bottles of milk.

But before the time when she was big enough to be ridden, she had what she considered to be big adventures. The old gray mare was expecting her third foal. She was probably twenty years old by then and shouldn't have been in such a condition. But Pancho, a big black colt I was boarding, had not yet been gelded and he and the gray mare had a romance.

I thought that the safest place to keep the old mare was in the yard around the house, which was Cherie's residence. By then Cherie was nearly half a year old and could be put out with the big horses. It wasn't as if they didn't know her. They had spent much time watching her across the fence. Nearly all adult horses are interested in young ones. Geldings seem especially fond of the young, and if a foal's mother will permit such attention, a gelding enjoys nuzzling the very young and watching over it while it sleeps.

Pepper, Pericles and Penny could think of nothing better than nosing Cherie, then taking her up over a hill to graze with them. I hoped that in their desire to be near her, to touch her, that they wouldn't frighten Cherie and make her run into a fence.

I needn't have worried. She was as eager to be with them as they were to be with her. She stretched her head toward theirs, moved her jaws in the funny up-and-down way a colt feels to be the thing to do when meeting its betters.

She climbed with the big horses to graze in a high meadow, but she came back, all of them following, when she grew thirsty for milk. By now her voice had recovered, she did not squawk. But still her whinny was a little strange; it seemed to carry the quality of her earlier efforts.

The gray mare liked it in the yard around the house, liked her buckets of water and all the good things I gave her to eat. I watched her anxiously as she grew larger and her udder swelled with milk ready to be used. One dawn I came halfway awake, heard the unmistakable low, soft sound of a mare speaking to her newborn. I must have been mixed up in a dream for I went back to sleep. But almost at once I was wide awake and tore out of the house.

The gray mare was being delighted over a little mouse-colored filly. So, also, were Cherie and her friends. They stood, big-eyed, peering over the fence, nostrils dilated to catch the sweet scent of the new one. The mare looked at them closely and got herself between them and the foal.

Obviously, there was nothing Cherie wanted more than another young one to play with. But she would have to wait until the foal was a little older, until the mare became less protective.

Later we named the little filly Periwinkle because, as she started to shed her baby coat, she was almost blue for a time. When she was older she turned shining black. But long before that time Cherie and she were allowed to be friends. I think that by then the mare was almost glad that there was someone besides herself for the foal to bite and kick.

Periwinkle was too formal a name and was reduced to Winkie. Whenever we called Cherie, Winkie came with her, and if I called Winkie, Cherie came to see what I wanted. Together they sprawled out in the sun, together they raced and bucked. But Winkie hurried to her mother for milk while Cherie rushed to me.

The spring that Cherie was two years old she stopped being a buckskin. Her old coat fell off and her new one was exactly the soft brown color of a deer.

When Winkie was three years old I trained her to be ridden, but I let Cherie wait another year. Even though I had tried to be a good mother, I couldn't be as good as a mare could be. Cherie wasn't completely full-grown until she was eight years old. Before that time, she had developed no withers so that her saddle slid forward if we went downhill. But at four years old she was big and strong enough to carry me on short rides, and I started her education.

When first I saddled her she minded not at all. She looked around and poked the stirrup with her nose. Cherie, even when she was very young, had always seemed wise. When first I got on her she turned her head to the left and looked back and up at me. She had last seen me on her left side as I stood on earth. Cherie's big, well-spaced eyes contributed to her look of wisdom. On that day, as she turned her head to regard my strange whereabouts, I looked into one eye and noticed once again its golden flecks which her sire had donated.

I picked up the reins and we started down the road. Cherie grew alarmed and bolted, but only for a brief distance. Then she settled down to a good swinging walk; when she jogged it was feathery-light. I'll always remember that first ride on her because it was so good.

Some years later there was another ride to remember. It was spring and Cherie felt hilarious. I had jumped on her bareback, with only a noose around her nose. I was galloping across a pasture to bring in some cows when Cherie's sudden high spirits nearly got the best of me. She leaped into the air, kicked up her heels, and swerved to the side. This left me completely out in space and I was ready for a hard landing on earth when Cherie suddenly swerved back under me. I was never so grateful for anything a horse ever did, even if, probably, it was not intentional.

My last ride on Cherie is another to be remembered. At that time I had a broken bone, due to Cherie's son, Cherokee, tossing me off when I least expected anything like that to happen. I could hobble out on crutches and saddle Cherie, I could get on her from the front steps. She was good about waiting for me to flounder into the saddle. But once up, I could not dismount because I had to leave my crutches where I'd mounted. I carried a rope which made it possible for me to open and shut gates. Cherie would wait for me to tie rope to gate, I'd swing it open, she'd step through, I'd pull it back and get it fastened. Then I'd untie the rope and carry it, for use in case we needed to go through another gate.

This day I was riding to bring home a young steer that had got out on a big cattle ranch adjoining ours. At that time Cherie was old, well along in her twenties, but she moved in her usual eager light-footed way. I enjoyed it as we rode here and there on the range, trying to find which bunch of cattle the steer had joined. Cherie seemed to enjoy it too. It was a day in early summer when the grass was golden and the oak trees were looking as bright as if it were still spring. There were wildflowers blooming out of the dry earth.

We found the steer with a small herd of white-faced creatures several miles from home. He did not want to leave his friends. He did not want to go home. It seems to be the custom of range cows to start running as soon as they see anyone on a horse, and this they did. Cherie had to run fast to get ahead of them and turn them back. Then she had to run fast again and rein quickly to cut out the steer and start him toward home. He was unwilling about doing any of this, and kept trying to turn back and outrun us.

Finally, after we managed to get him away from the others, he would evade us enough to hide in thick clumps of chaparral into which no horse could be ridden. Had I been able to dismount and walk, I could have scared him out by throwing stones and yelling, but this I couldn't do. All I could do was to rein Cherie as far into the brush as she could make it, yelling as I went.

Once we got him out, Cherie had to travel fast to keep him from hiding again, and to keep him going in the direction of home. It was hard work for her, but she never slowed or even showed signs that she wanted to rest. She seemed to feel as intense about getting that steer home as I did, and finally we succeeded.

The next day I looked at Cherie and felt like the meanest person on earth. She was so stiff, sore and lame she could scarcely walk. I fed her a good breakfast and hugged her and promised I'd never ride her again.

I kept my promise, even though in a few days she seemed completely recovered. Now she is over thirty years old and is as happy and well fed as any old mare can be.

But with spring in the air I wouldn't jump on her bareback with only a rope to hold her, and gallop across the grass. Suddenly she might cavort and toss me sky-high. I would be delighted with her spirit, but not with what could happen to me.

WINKIE
AND PEPPER

All three of the gray mare's colts were good horses. Perhaps the last-born, the black filly Winkie, was the best. She was very quick. She was quick to learn and she was quick when she moved. When I mounted her I had to be quick too. I'd put a foot in the stirrup and make a dive for the saddle, for Winkie would be moving either backward, forward, or to the side. You'd think she didn't want to be ridden and was going to start bucking like anything, but she never bucked, and somehow I never missed finding the saddle. But one day, when I was riding an English saddle, suddenly she started trotting backwards. This put me on her neck, which startled her so that somehow, quickly, she sat down, exactly like a dog.

I like to remember how, one black night, she brought me out of the hills. Ordinarily, when you are outdoors as night comes on, your eyes adjust so that the night never seems completely black and you can see where you go. But this was an extra-black night to begin with, and then, back in the hills, we had been sitting around the light of a cook fire. So when I mounted Winkie I could not see her black ears. I could not see the trail at all, or even where it should be. I rode her with a loose rein and she walked with quick, firm steps, stopping from time to time to put her nose right down to the earth, to make sure. My pride in her grew stronger with every step she took.

One time a hunter, shooting near, scared her so that she ran and got a bad barbed-wire cut. And later she ran away, played over a barbed-wire fence with another mare, struck out quickly with one front hoof, and gave herself such a wire cut that there was no use trying to ride her after it healed. She was sure to go lame.

But, out in pasture, she was scarcely lame at all. Unless she was trotting fast you didn't notice it. I knew she would make a wonderful brood mare.

Pepper, the gray mare's first-born, was very beautiful. For a time his summer coat was dark gray and his winter coat buckskin. Later he turned dapple gray. He had black and white hairs in his tail and his mane was black. His dark eyes were big, his head like that of an Arabian. For a while, when his brother Pericles turned the same color, I had a matched pair, as to color anyway. Pericles was chunkier and not quite so pretty.

Pepper was a good horse to ride and good at gymkhana games. He enjoyed playing musical chairs. Though he was gentle and easy to manage, I used to fall off him frequently, especially in very warm weather. He wasn't overly lively on a hot day. He trudged along half asleep, with me drowsy and droopy in the saddle. In his half-dormant state any sudden sound or sight would startle him so that, all at once, he'd give a convulsive jump and leap right out from under me. He had a charming personality and was affectionate and fond of people.

Late one summer Pepper suddenly began to act strange. He moved slowly, he dragged his feet when he walked. The vet said it was evident he had had a case of sleeping sickness, but a very light one. There was a slight chance that he might recover.

Pepper's wits had left him. He behaved as one in a daze, and he grew thin. He lived up in the hills with the other horses. On the ranch there was a hill behind the house and I liked to watch the line of horses run down the winding trail on their way home to drink. They waited until they were very thirsty and then they came charging down, a great dust cloud behind them.

One day I saw Winkie stop suddenly when she was about halfway down. The others went streaming past her excitedly, but she stood stock-still. Winkie was waiting for Pepper. She had waited patiently for him for about half an hour when he appeared, moving in his slow way, and they came down the hill together. After that, I noticed that always Winkie waited for her brother. Sometimes she went back after him and brought him to drink. No matter how thirsty she might be, or how eager to race downhill with the others, she waited. It must have been a hard thing for her to do, for it is against horse nature

to stand still while other horses are running.

While she grazed she would keep an eye on him, as if he were her little colt, and sometimes he, right in the middle of his own pasture, would get lost and whinny wildly. Winkie would answer, then trot briskly after him. She assumed complete charge, so I did not need to bother about him at all. She made a point of bringing him to water and to the salt lick, and she would take him to graze where the grass was best. Her black face wore a sweet and wise expression as she watched over him.

Still he grew thinner, and, as time went on, it was evident that he would never be normal. It wasn't until we planned to move from one ranch to another that we decided it would be better if Pepper were dead. We reasoned that the change to new pastures would take Winkie's mind off him. She loved him and cared for him so well that we couldn't have parted them if we had continued on the old ranch. But there was no way to move Pepper. He couldn't travel many miles on his own hoofs, and it was too dangerous to put a deranged horse in a trailer where he might throw himself around and be badly hurt. Besides, we were planning to let Winkie become a mother and then she'd forget all about poor Pepper.

When the veterinary came with his lethal needle we put Winkie in a stall and gave her hay to keep her mind off Pepper a while. We led Pepper to a meadow, out of sight, but, sadly, not out of sound, so that, until he became unconscious, Pepper was whinnying for Winkie and she was calling to him. He never looked more beautiful, more alive, than he did at the moment before his eyes dimmed.

COLLEEN

Collen was not mine. She belonged to my friend Myrtle who lived near me. But I knew and loved Colleen so well that she too became a part of the herd of horses I seemed to have inherited from the gray mare.

There wasn't a chance that the old mare, Babe, would have a pinto colt. She was bay and the foal's sire was a chestnut thoroughbred. Yet when the little filly was born she was a red and white pinto, gay as a stick of peppermint candy—and as peppery. With all her heart Myrtle had longed for a pinto and she'd actually prayed for one. She stared and stared at the little red and white blob that looked like a rocking horse. Here indeed was a miracle. The foal was soon on her feet, staggering about, exploring the wide world. Myrtle named her Colleen.

When Colleen was about six weeks old we were bringing her and her mother in from pasture to put them in a
small corral for the night. The corral was up on a hill and
Colleen skipped gayly up the trail ahead of us. Then she
spotted, a few feet from the corral gate, something fas-
cinating. Mama goose was sitting on some eggs and the
gander was standing guard. Colleen poked her little nose
toward these interesting specimens of poultry life. Papa
goose let out a loud honk and Colleen whirled, headed
elsewhere. But the gander seized her fluffy tail and held
on, beating her with his wings. No little filly ever ran
faster. She not only ran, from time to time she gave a
leap, which, with the gander's wings flapping, gave her
the appearance of a horse ready to fly: At every jump

she squealed for her mother or for us to come quickly and save her. Her mother responded, pulling the lead rope from my hand, racing after her child, while I raced after her — and two mother geese, enthusiastic about excitement, raced after us.

Colleen hit the fence at the foot of the hill and slid through. This was too much for the gander; he hadn't counted on a barbed-wire entanglement. Anyway, he had saved his unhatched goslings. He strutted back to meet his wives and they all clapped their wings and laughed at the top of their voices.

While Babe, Myrtle and I were trying to get little Colleen back on her own side of the fence she got in too big of a hurry and scratched herself on the barbed wire. The wire made a furrow down the full length of her back. Later, the hair grew in white, making a long narrow stripe which she wore all her life. She never grew fond of geese.

That curious little nose of hers was bound to get Colleen into more trouble. She soon had another adventure associated with poultry, though remotely. The little yellow hen had hatched all of her eggs but two and these Myrtle had placed in a wheelbarrow full of trash, to be dumped later. But Colleen got there first. Myrtle stared at her in amazement, not knowing what was wrong. A streak of red and white ran to some loose plowed earth, a small nose tried to bury itself in the dirt. She tried to spit, she wrinkled up her nose, she pawed. Clouds of dust encircled her. She shook her head and struck at her nose with both front hoofs. So frantic was she that Myrtle was sure she'd been bitten by a snake. Suddenly as a last resort, she ran straight to Myrtle for help, and tried to rub her nose against her. Immediately Myrtle knew what the trouble was. Colleen was saturated with the strong smell of rotten eggs! She wanted to run away from that smell, to fight it off somehow. She even fought Myrtle as she got a rope on her and went to work trying to get her clean. It took buckets of soapy water, with disinfectant added, before the little filly could like herself again. That was the last time Colleen ever tried eggs.

As summer progressed we had more and more bott flies, those bee-like insects that buzz and buzz around the horses to lay eggs on their coats. All horses run wildly from bott flies; even the smallest colts are annoyed by the angry buzzing. Colleen was not very old before she figured out a wonderful escape, which was to make a quick dash for her mother, duck down, and dash under her mother's belly and out the other side. She would be halfway across the pasture and still going strong before the old mare realized that now *she* was playing hostess to the bott fly! Years later, when she was full-grown, Colleen would always contrive some way to wish off a bott fly on another horse.

Her first taste of corn fodder was a shock to her. The cornstalks were dry and rattly and when Colleen eagerly picked the leaf of a big stalk and began chewing, the rustling startled her so that she jumped in the air, and, still holding the cornstalk in her mouth, made a dash for mama, hoping to pull the bott fly trick successfully. With the cornstalk dragging after her, she ducked under Babe's belly, which frightened Babe too. They both raced off to

the open spaces, Colleen with her teeth clenched on
the cornstalk. The faster she ran the more it rattled
and slapped her legs. She slid to a stop, whirled round and
round on her hind legs like a ballet dancer, faster and
faster. The stalk broke loose and flew to one side and she
collapsed on her haunches, whinnying loudly for her
mother to save her. Babe trotted anxiously to her and
the little one tried standing up. It was as bad as the first
time she had ever found her legs, when she was newborn. She wobbled this way and that, dizzy and weak,
shaking with fright and exhaustion. She was covered with
sweat. But she had learned something. From that time on,
whenever she was fed corn fodder, she would put one
front foot firmly on the stalk and hold it down before
she'd take her first bite. But old Babe wasn't that smart;
she continued to scare herself every time she was served
a stalk.

Little colts need hills to climb and wide places to run
in order to develop strong muscles and good wind. So
Myrtle decided to turn Babe and Colleen out in a hill
pasture with some big work horses, owned by an old
man called Fred. There were eleven of them, all fat and
sleek. The youngest was ten years old and she was the
last foal that the others could remember ever having seen,
and she herself had never seen a baby horse. We led Babe
and little Colleen into the new place before the bunch of
horses saw us. They came charging down the hills, their
big hoofs shaking the earth. It was like an avalanche
descending on us, all those big horses, tons of them, intent
upon investigating this small member of their tribe.

They circled like a band of Indians, and kept getting closer. In her excitement, one of the biggest mares jumped and whirled, lost her footing, fell and rolled completely over. She scrambled back to her big clumsy hoofs and rushed toward the small filly. None of the horses wanted to harm Colleen; it was only that they were curious and excited, but with so many big hoofs flying about there was danger for both Colleen and Babe. Babe had her ears back flat, her teeth bared, and she was plunging and kicking. Colleen moved right up beside her mother's chest and chewed the air vigorously, as colts do in moments of excitement. She was begging to be left alone. The big ones closed in, striking and squealing and kicking at one another. There was no fighting them back, even though we swatted at them with ropes and threw rocks and yelled.

We were too far from the gate to escape. There seemed to be only one thing to do—turn the mare and foal free to fend for themselves. With Colleen glued tight to her side, Babe dashed through an opening she had spotted in the circle of horses. The two raced up a hillside with all the big horses lumbering after them, but it was a case of plow horses trying to capture Pegasus. Mare and foal bounded over the hill like a doe and fawn, while we stood below, shaking with fear for their safety.

We mounted our saddle horses and rode to the highest peak where we could get a good view in every direction —and then we saw that we had nothing to worry about. Babe, being very wise, had slipped into a little hidden cove with her baby. The two kept very quiet while the

big horses thundered by. The herd circled around for awhile, baffled, then went back to the barn. There they smelled the ground, nosing the small hoof prints, until finally they gave up, feeling, no doubt, that the small one had actually taken wing and flown.

For several days after that Babe watched from a high point until the other horses had drunk and gone out to graze, then she and Colleen sneaked down to the spring to drink. But gradually she relaxed her vigil. All the horses grew accustomed to one another and little Colleen became the pride of the pasture. Babe had plenty of baby-sitters. All the mares helped take care of the filly; they switched off flies and kept coyotes away. They took almost too good care of her. When we would go over to the pasture to see how she and her mother were getting along, they would try to take her off and hide her in the hills. They nipped her lightly, whinnied at her and pawed. They tried every way they knew to make her run off with them. But Colleen liked to be admired and petted, and she was fond of the grain we might be bringing to her, so she and her mother would run to meet us. The big horses would then attempt to herd them back, getting between them and us, and little Colleen would peek anxiously from under thick necks and around fat rumps.

One big brown mare would charge straight at us, her ears tight back. With her head shaking and her long black mane flowing, she looked furious, but it was all bluff. She wished she could chase us away from that foal, but we wouldn't chase. Finally, Babe and Colleen would find an opening in the horseflesh wall and rush toward us.

All the time we were visiting, the foster parents would stand watchfully by, waiting for the moment we would leave. Then they'd herd the mare and colt back to the hills, with many furtive glances over their shoulders to make sure we were actually leaving.

But no matter how protective they were, nothing was going to protect Colleen from her own curiosity. One morning her nose investigated a pretty little black and white animal, and there was sudden catastrophe. From a distance a skunk smell is not so bad, but close up it is strong and gassy, indescribably offensive, and painful to eyes and nose. The encounter with the skunk was far worse than the adventure with the rotten eggs. After it, Colleen flung herself down to roll in the dirt, kicked and pawed and squealed, and then tried to rub herself on old Babe. Her eyes stung and watered and her nose dripped. For several days she was not popular with her friends. She realized with dismay that they were not playing at being race horses when they flung up their heels and galloped away whenever she ran toward them.

But, instinctively, she was not curious about rattle-snakes. Also, her mother had taught her to leave them alone. One day Myrtle was riding the old mare, with Colleen tagging along, up over the pasture hill. They were on a narrow trail along a ledge when Babe and Myrtle saw, right there before them, the biggest red rattlesnake either had ever seen. It was coiled into a mound that must have been a foot and a half high. Babe screamed and jumped before Myrtle could realize what was happening. The three went together over a cliff, landing right-

side up some eight feet below, where they shivered and
shook for awhile before they felt like moving again. Colleen and Babe did some fearsome snorting along with
their shaking. Not all horses are afraid of snakes and
Myrtle was glad that this small one had learned early to
avoid them.

Fred, the owner of the big work horses, was a kindly
old-timer who lived alone. His only family consisted of
those beautiful big animals. To him each of the horses
was a beloved personality, and of course no two were
alike. Some worked so eagerly that they danced ahead
of the plow, some were pokey and slow, but all were
willing to do their share of the work that kept the ranch
going. None were worked too long or too hard, and all of
them had long vacations from time to time, out in the hill
pasture.

The biggest horse we'd ever seen was old Sam, who
had a great long head which his owner said looked as if
it had been hung on upside down. Sam was especially
fond of small Colleen; he was like an adoring old uncle.
Colleen would tease him, nipping his huge rump and
whirling around to let fly with both hind heels, drum-
ming away on his side with all her might. She chewed on
his mane and pulled his tail, and, when his head was low
enough, bit his ears. He followed her adoringly, wanting
more pestering. The mares were just as bad, regarding
every mischievous act of the filly lovingly, all fighting for
the chance to touch her with their big gentle noses. Fred
watched his horses and decided that if they were made
that happy by a young one, he'd raise some colts. So the

next year two of the mares foaled and the herd was happy with its own colts, all because Colleen had lived there awhile.

For most foals, weaning time is a sad ordeal. When Colleen was big enough to do without her mother, and old Babe was growing thin from producing so much milk, it was time to separate them. We threw out armloads of hay to keep the work horses and Colleen occupied, then we hurried old Babe home, much against her will. She worried for some days about Colleen, and Colleen did some whinnying for her, but actually she didn't seem to miss her mother very much. She had all the big friendly work horses to keep her from being too lonely. Grass was good and, though she missed the sweet taste of milk, she had plenty to eat.

Colleen grew in size and strength. She would race up and down the steep hillsides, dodging between rocks and trees at top speed. This taught her to be sure-footed so that, in later years, she could chase cattle over the roughest country and be as nimble as a deer.

Winter was upon us again and it was time for Colleen to leave the hills and join Babe in the home corral. They hadn't forgotten each other, but now their relationship had changed. They were good friends instead of being mother and daughter. When we started to bring Colleen home, all the big horses tried to break the gate and follow, so we had to lead her back to the barn and wait while Fred tied some of them up and threw out hay to keep the others interested. For the next few days they whinnied and searched for her, unable to realize that she had really gone away.

Colleen's coat did not grow very heavy in the fall; it remained fine and silky so that when rains came and cold winds blew she shivered. Myrtle made her a blanket out of feed sacks and bundled her into it whenever the weather was bad. Colleen wasn't the only one who liked her feed-sack blanket. A small black kitten had become her friend and it soon discovered that Colleen, wearing her blanket, was a cozy spot for sleeping. From the top rail of the fence it would leap to Colleen's rump where it would curl up and go warmly to sleep. Colleen always seemed to be careful, if she moved about, not to dislodge her kitten. And when she lay down to nap, the little cat would either be on her or close beside her. Compared to the kitten, Colleen was very large and, had she been careless, she could have injured it easily. But she knew better than to step on it or roll on it. Sometimes the kitten rubbed against her affectionately, purring, as kittens like to do. Colleen would stand with her chin over the fence rail and the kitten would walk back and forth underneath it, giving Colleen a delightful sensation as it rubbed the underside of her chin. The two would indulge in this enjoyable occupation for an hour at a time, each looking very happy.

Colleen had dog friends too, a German shepherd named Baron, and a little fox terrier called Zip. Baron and Colleen were almost inseparable. They'd play together, running races across the pasture, and, while Colleen grazed, Baron would curl up and go to sleep in the grass. Together they'd drive out any strange dogs that came into the pasture,

Colleen striking and squealing, Baron barking and growling, so that the intruders left in a hurry, sorry they'd ever thought of stopping by.

When Colleen was big enough, Myrtle started getting her used to saddle and hackamore. The filly didn't really mind; she was only a trifle surprised at first, then turned to nose the swinging stirrups of the saddle. When Myrtle put Zip, the fox terrier, up in the saddle Colleen didn't object to giving her friend a ride. She was still not big enough to carry Myrtle's weight for very long, so Myrtle didn't stay on her for more than ten minutes a day. Myrtle taught her a little about how to rein to the right and left, and she was quick to learn. When spring came again she had had enough lessons for one her age and size, so she could go back to the hill pasture to spend the summer with her work horse friends.

BUCK

I first met Buck one summer afternoon when I was riding down a road toward San Diego. I was on the gray mare's first colt, Pepper. A girl on a buckskin horse came riding up beside me, headed in the same direction. Naturally, we traveled along together and started to talk. The girl, tall, lean and blonde, was named Mardy, and the horse, being a buckskin, naturally was called Buck.

Buck and Pepper looked at each other with intense interest. They would have liked to stop and smell noses, which, I suppose, is a type of horse conversation. They probably felt they could learn something about each other in this fashion.

I told Mardy where I lived, outside the city on a ranch not far from the road we were following. Mardy told me that, alas, she lived in the city but that there was a

canyon near her house where she could keep Buck. She and Buck had been spending her vacation at a summer place in the mountains, but now she had to take him back to the city because she had to go to school. Sometime, she said, she and Buck were going to live on a ranch. She thought I was lucky to have already escaped the city.

I looked at Buck and thought him very pretty. He arched his neck and traveled proudly. He was almost golden, but his mane, tail and socks were jet black, a contrast that added to his handsome appearance. He moved with such liveliness that I voiced by admiration for so spirited a horse.

Mardy sighed. "He isn't spirited, really. He's acting so because there is another horse along. As soon as you leave us he will begin to plod. Buck is a very odd horse. He goes well only when he feels like it."

At last it came time for me to turn back toward home. As Mardy rode on I heard despairing whinnies from Buck. He didn't want to have to go the rest of the way without another horse companion. Pepper answered him, but then Pepper was glad to hurry on because he was returning to home and hay.

I did not see Mardy and Buck again for some time. One day, however, Mardy and her father came driving up to my house. "We've come about Buck," Mardy explained. "I have to go away to school and there will be no one to take care of him. We wondered if you could board him for me. We would pay you, of course."

I, in my innocence, agreed.

Some days later a teen-age girl came riding up to the

barn on Buck. She announced herself as Mardy's sister Jane. She said that she had brought Buck to stay.

We put him in the corral by the barn and he trotted about and whinnied at the horses who were wandering around. Soon Jane's father came driving up to take her back to the city. As they were leaving, Jane said, "I hope you'll get along with Buck all right."

"Oh, sure," I replied carelessly. Little did I realize that Buck, in some ways, was to be the worst horse I had ever met in my entire life. And also the most interesting.

The first time I ever put a rope around his neck and tried to lead him, I found out immediately that this wasn't the way to do it. Buck started going at a good rate of speed in the direction he chose to go, dragging me along, helpless to control him. After that, I learned to slip a noose around his nose because, that way, he had not so much pulling power.

I thought I might ride Buck a short distance and attempt to teach him some manners. When I started to bridle him he objected—with two front hoofs and a head waving around high in the air. I struggled until I, but not Buck, was tired out. Then I had an idea. I went into the house, took a slice of bread and wrapped it around his bit. Buck opened his mouth and accepted bit and bread. Later I learned that this was Mardy's way of coping with the same situation.

Buck didn't mind having a saddle slung on him, he didn't object to being cinched up. He stood quietly while I mounted. I picked up the reins, kicked him with my heels— and he stood calmly, his four hoofs firm upon the earth.

I removed the quirt from my saddle horn and gave him a good whack over the rump. This put him into motion, but not forward. He merely stayed in the same place and kicked up his heels. I seemed to be more in motion than he was.

Since this was one of the times when I felt myself growing as determined as any animal, I kept gathering the reins, kicking with my heels, and whacking a buckskin rump. After Buck decided that it wasn't doing him any good to remain in one spot kicking up his heels, he moved forward. Suddenly, interested in learning his destination, he changed from a slow plod to a springy jog. I began to enjoy him.

Presently I dismounted and opened a gate leading into a big cattle ranch. After I mounted again Buck stood, looking dreamy and inactive. We went through the same process again. I gathered him, kicked with my heels, whacked his rump. He removed his hind hoofs from the ground and returned to the same spot. After enough determined effort on my part, he again moved forward, but not with any degree of swiftness.

We traveled toward a pretty spot not far from the gate. Here there was a sweet little pasture pond, bordered by reeds, where redwing blackbirds swung and made the most beautiful music. When Buck smelled the water, his steps quickened. I thought he must be thirsty and let him put his head down to drink. He didn't drink. He waded into the pond and put his head down again. In spite of all my pulling on the reins, yelling, kicking with my heels and whacking with the quirt, Buck bent his knees and went down for a comforting roll in the sun-warmed water.

I leaped off, promptly got soaked, jerked the reins and dragged Buck to shore. Saddle, blanket and bridle were as wet as I. Buck was soaked too, but looked smug and pleased.

On dry land I squished myself into the saddle and this time Buck started off happily. Toward home he broke into a swinging gallop that was a delight to ride. As he loped along he kept uttering breathless whinnies. He was in a hurry to get home and to the other horses.

At that time I happened to be boarding another young horse, a red and white pinto named Patches. Patches had arrived at the age where he considered himself a ferocious stallion. It was his delight to try to fight every gelding he saw. If I rode a horse through the small pasture where Patches lived, Patches, ears back flat and teeth bared, gave chase. This was a problem.

One day I thought I had the solution. I got on my little strawberry roan, Johnny, took a long buggy whip and rode into Patches' pasture. When he started to chase us my plan was to swing around and whip him.

It didn't work at all. Johnny became so terrified that he ran for his life and I could not slow him or turn him. Patches was gnawing on his rump and Johnny was accelerating his speed. All I could do was to stay with the fast journey, around and around, until both animals tired enough to slow down. Then I jumped off Johnny and tried to beat Patches back until I could get poor Johnny safely out the gate. He was trembling with terror and exhaustion.

It was Buck who gave me the idea of how to reform

Patches. Horses usually have such firm attachments to their own home range that a new horse introduced to a pasture has a bad time of it. My horses have been known to chase a new one right through a fence.

But when Buck first met with my horses he was not in the least intimidated. He was willing to kick or bite any horse that wanted to chase him away. Very soon he was accepted because he had to be. Buck wasn't going to have it otherwise.

I finally decided to put him in the same pasture with Patches and let Buck, who seemed to have no manners himself, teach Patches manners. Immediately Patches came charging toward Buck, indicating in every possible way that he was going to tear him apart. Buck simply stared. Patches, astonished that Buck was not running away, stopped and stared back. Then Buck strode to Patches, stretched out his neck, reached to smell noses in a friendly way. With that, Patches whirled to kick and Buck dodged. Patches reared to strike with a front hoof and Buck ducked out of the way. Ears flat, Patches tore into him.

Buck seemed to be saying, "Well, this is it. I'm sorry." He gave the impression of one calmly rolling up his sleeves and going to work.

For the first time in his life, Patches got a complete and thorough trouncing. Buck kicked, struck, bit. Patches was never so surprised. When the dust settled Patches had only a few skinned places, Buck had not a hair out of place. Patches had enormous respect. After that, I turned Patches out with the other horses and he never tried to fight again. Buck was there to see that he didn't.

I found solace in remembering how Buck had settled Patches when, later, Buck caused me all kinds of trouble. He was always getting over, under or through fences, going to neighbors' gardens, making everyone mad at me for harboring him.

Once I read a book which said that one thing a horse will never do is to crawl or creep under a fence. The author didn't know Buck!

Sometimes when I rode Buck he was the best horse I ever rode and sometimes he was the worst.

I was to learn later that Buck was to Mardy what the old gray mare was to me. Buck's hoofs eventually carried her to ranch country of her own, to other wonderful horses. But none of them was ever like Buck.

Years later Mardy, who became one of my best friends, said to me, "I used to wonder why you put up with Buck all the time I was in school. Wherever I'd had him boarded before it never worked. Somebody would notify me to come and take him away at once."

I said, "It never occurred to me to tell you to come and

get him or I would have. I just thought I was stuck with him. And then your father paid his board bill regularly . . ."

When Mardy first got Buck he had been ridden only about three times. He didn't know any more about being ridden than Mardy knew about riding. They both had to learn together. Mardy turned out to be one of the best riders I know, and before old age finally overtook him, Buck became (at times) a reasonably good horse.

Buck was always a horse of distinction. He had his own opinions about everything—and all of them were rigid.

Though he was still young when he came to stay with me, he had had many adventures. Because Mardy had such a hard time finding a place for him during the school year, once, at the end of a summer vacation, in desperation she did what no one should ever do to a loved horse. She got Buck a job at a rent stable where he could earn his own room and board. Rent horses usually have a bad time of it, since the majority of people who hire them know little or nothing about riding.

In this case, however, Mardy knew that the stable to which Buck was going was a reliable place. The horses were fed well there and the proprietor did his best to see that they were not ridden too hard. Added to this, Mardy also knew that Buck had a great capacity for looking after himself. She didn't have to worry. No one was going to ride Buck too far or too hard.

Very quickly Buck proved Mardy right. Before he had lived a week at the stable he had found a way out. Whenever he was ridden, he would docilely trudge along for perhaps half a mile. Then he would suddenly lie down and groan. He went down slowly and mournfully so that his rider had time to remove himself. This was not consideration on Buck's part. Buck was not concerned with what happened to the rider.

A thoughtful rider might tie his reins to a bush, if Buck had been absent-minded enough to lie down beside one. Other people simply hurried back to the riding stable on foot to report a sick horse. By the time the stable man went to find him, Buck would be up and grazing—and not easily caught. Always Buck's timing was perfect. He was a master at waiting until the last moment to dodge away from a reaching hand.

Buck spent some lovely months being a rent horse because soon the word got around and no one would hire him. All that Buck had to do was to stand about and dream until feeding time. But of course it didn't pay the stable to keep a fattening horse which no one wanted to rent.

Tales about Buck's exploits have become legendary. One of the funniest involved a long-time friend of Mardy's named Ginnie. Though the years have passed, Ginnie tells about it to this day, not without bitterness.

Mardy and Ginnie were attending high school in San Diego. One day Mardy found that she had to stay late after classes and she suggested that Ginnie give Buck his afternoon ride. Ginnie was delighted and felt flattered and important as she walked down to Buck's canyon corral. Buck permitted himself to be saddled, though he protested against the bridle. But Ginnie had provided for this contingency. She had bread and sugar lumps in her pocket and she wrapped the bread around the bit as she'd seen

Mardy do. Then, by way of reward, she fed Buck the sugar.

At first Buck traveled well. But when they reached the valley below his home, Ginnie turned Buck to the right and the horse decided he wanted to go in the other direction. Ginnie pulled and gave him a whack with her quirt. Buck ducked his head and kicked up his heels. Ginnie grabbed at his mane, but went sailing over his head. Being a determined young lady, she continued to hold onto the reins while she sat in the dusty road.

A motorist stopped, got out of his car, and helped Ginnie up.

"I want to get on again," she said bravely.

"Oh, I wouldn't," the man advised.

Ginnie insisted and the man lifted her into the saddle. Almost at once Buck threw her. Again she kept tight hold of the reins so that Buck could not run away.

"I've got to ride home," Ginnie insisted, and, against his better judgment, the man helped her up again. At once the earth revolved dizzily beneath her and Ginnie rushed to meet it.

"Had enough?" asked the man.

Painfully, Ginnie got to her feet and started leading Buck toward home. The horse watched the seat of her jeans moving ahead of him. He was fascinated. He stretched out his neck and took a mouthful of blue denim. He enjoyed the result. Ginnie yelped and jumped forward.

Home after a ride meant hay, and Buck was in a hurry. Every now and then he tried to rush Ginnie along by giving her a poke with his nose. At last she turned to slap his face, but he ducked in time and seized her jeans again.

Ginnie tried running, but when she did Buck lagged and pulled back on the reins. If she walked at a moderate rate of speed he stretched out his neck and bit. When she tired walking backward he acted as if she planned to beat him. His eyes rolled, he snorted, and he would not come.

Finally, the two of them got to the city streets and Mardy's neighborhood. There Ginnie met with even more embarrassment. The neighborhood children, always fascinated with Buck and his adventures, came running. "What's the matter, Ginnie? You scared to ride him?" they called.

Ginnie tried to ignore the children, but she was to suffer still further humiliation. It was the hour when people were watering their lawns and inevitably wasting water. Water crossed sidewalks, flowed onto streets. Not deeply, just a thin layer of water crossing pavement.

Buck indicated that he would rather die than to get his hoofs wet. He stopped, snorted, braced himself. Ginnie could neither pull nor push him across a wet bit of street.

Ginnie turned back, tried another street—and met with the same problem.

Poor Ginnie tried street after street—up one, down another, before she got Buck safely home. Nearly every street was wet. Buck objected at every crossing.

Ginnie and Buck arrived at Mardy's house, Ginnie breathless and angry. Mardy registered surprise. Ginnie didn't even speak to her. She glowered for a moment, then walked away.

Anyone used to horses might think that Buck was a

worthless, badly spoiled young horse. In some ways he was, but in other ways he wasn't. When Mardy rode him she made him be a good horse. It was just that Buck was intelligent enough to judge his rider. A person who didn't handle him properly got the worst of it.

One time when Mardy and Buck were living in the mountains where Mardy worked in summer vacation, Buck showed a noble side to his nature. He saved the life of a mare named Kitten.

Mardy had been busy that particular morning and had let a little boy take Buck and Kitten to be tied on long ropes in grass down by a creek bed.

An hour later, Buck began whinnying so urgently and loudly that Mardy thought Kitten must have broken loose and run away. Buck had grown attached to the mare and was sure to complain if they were separated. Mardy rushed to investigate. Buck was plunging at the end of his rope. He was covered with sweat and lather and he continued to shout at the top of his voice.

Kitten was there all right. She was on the ground, thrashing her legs, and she was fighting to breathe. The little boy had tied her with a slip knot and Kitten was strangling to death. Frantically, Mardy tried to undo the knot but it was pulled too tight. She ran to get a knife to cut Kitten free. By the time she got back she thought the mare was dead. Buck screamed and plunged as Mardy sawed the rope free from Kitten's throat.

As soon as pressure was removed, Kitten began to come back to life. But she sounded as if each breath gave her pain. Finally, weak and wobbly, she got to her feet.

Buck stopped his wild cries and stared at her. Then, as unconcerned as if nothing had happened, he began enjoying his grass again.

He seemed to have no idea that he had done a very unusual thing. He was amazed when Mardy rushed to him to hug him and tell him he was the greatest horse on earth.

SHARON'S
LITTLE SISTER

Lambs we have had in October, calves in November, but never before have we had a foal when it wasn't spring. A young foal and a spring day go so perfectly together. It didn't seem likely that a foal would know how to be a foal unless it arrived at the time of green grass.

However, for years and years the sixteen-year-old mare, Nicky, had been producing a new foal every fall and many of her children had come to be well known as blue ribbon winners. So, apparently, a fall foal doesn't miss the bird song and grass scents the spring foals first know.

When, one February, Nicky came to live on my ranch, she had with her the October foal, Sharon. After Sharon grew old enough to have no need for her mother she still liked being with her. When a fence separated them she spent a great deal of time gossiping over the fence. So it

*Reprinted by permission of *The Christian Science Monitor*.

happened that Sharon saw her little sister before I did. One morning I went into the kitchen to drink a glass of milk, just after I'd finished doing early chores. I glanced toward the corral, noticed Sharon by the fence as usual, and her mother eating hay. In less than ten minutes I came out of the house, glanced toward the corral again, and— surely there was a tiny creature there!

As yet it hadn't stood up, but when I reached it, it stood up just like a grown horse. It didn't have to ponder about its long legs and how to arrange them, it scarcely wobbled. It got right up and started running. Its mother had to trot to keep up with it.

Friends came to visit the little foal. Everybody agreed that they'd never seen such a newborn one. Neither, apparently, had any of the horses that gathered around the fence to look at her. For this little one didn't want to stop and rest. All that first day she kept going, exploring the vast world of the corral, staring at people, staring at horses, staring at trees and earth and sky. All the foals I'd known before had lain down many times during their first day to sleep deeply. This one had too much to see. I got up in the middle of the night and went to look for her. She wasn't down yet. It wasn't until the next evening that we saw her lie down, finally, and then she got right up again.

She had a wide white blaze down her face and when I first saw her, with the sun shining on her, I nearly named her Sunflower. But it didn't quite fit. Once I nearly named her Polly because she was so talkative. Every time she saw me she said "He-he-he." Every time she saw another horse she spoke to it; she whinnied at the dogs, the cow, the sheep. Her Arabian sire, Algiers, was so noisy that he has been nicknamed Canary. Perhaps, I thought, I should name his daughter after a bird.

The foal had three white socks and one silver sock, her coat was bright chestnut, her mane was red and her tail was flaxen. Her neck was a soft curve, her straight back was short, as an Arabian's should be, her head was pure Arabian. An Arabian name, I thought? But none came to mind. So we called her "it," we called her "filly," and she didn't care whether we called her anything. The crisp weather inspired her so that she wanted to play wild horse. With her pale tail held high, she frolicked around the corral. She tried, ever and ever so many times, to jump clear away from her own shadow. She couldn't understand how anything else could be as swift as she was. At night the shadows were best. I turned on the corral light to make a giant shadow for her to race. It was her very favorite shadow and she had more fun with it than with any daytime shadow. Then came moonlight nights and we very nearly named her Moon-gold.

It was in the moonlight that she learned to lead. I had planned to halter her for the first time one particular day but somehow I hadn't gotten around to it. Under the bright harvest moon she learned about a rope. Almost, I felt sorry. I always do. To restrain anything so free and wild as a young foal, even for a brief time, seems almost like clipping the wings of Pegasus. But, in a way, I thought, a halter and lead rope would give the foal more freedom, for I could ride Nicky and lead her on short trips into the world beyond the corral.

The rope she did not like. Instead of fighting against it in the ordinary way, she kept poking me earnestly with her nose. She was saying, "Take this off." But I wouldn't. There was pressure on the rope, to take away the pressure she must follow. So, she reasoned, do it quickly. Make a big leap. So she leaped as far as she could, trying to reach me and the hand that would caress her.

Before she learned that she could follow at a walk or a jog she was nearly named Grasshopper.

All this time the foal's sister, Sharon, had been realizing that this little one had a great deal to do with herself and her mother. Sharon had never stopped yearning for the companionship of her mother. Now she continued to stay by the fence to watch the new one too. All she received from her mother was a very cross look but it didn't discourage her.

One day Sharon and every other loose horse on the ranch were penned up so that Nicky and the foal wouldn't be distracted when I took them out for the foal's first trip abroad. The little one wore her colt halter and lead rope.

Nicky, whom I rode bareback, wore a bridle, and, with the foal protesting about being hampered by a rope, we started forth. Out in the big world the foal forgot that she had ever learned to lead. She braced herself with all her strength.

Suddenly I heard a triumphant whinny, a sound of galloping hoofs. Sharon had leaped the fence. Now, thought I, remembering Nicky's cross looks at Sharon, Nicky will be upset and the foal won't learn anything. Hoofbeats behind her startled the foal into a wild struggle to escape, and, while she was rearing and plunging and pulling, Sharon joined us. I was expecting Nicky to let fly with hind heels.

Instead, she said something. Immediately, both her daughters stood statue-still. Then, ever so gently, Sharon touched her little sister. It was what she had been longing to do all the time. Standing as tall as she possibly could, the month-old foal lifted her head to the yearling. Happily, Nicky nosed them both. There was a beautiful moment when three heads of assorted sizes were close together. Then we started on our journey.

The foal had no more protests to make. She trotted gaily along the trail, safely sandwiched between her mother and her big sister, feeling every bit as wise as they.

TONY

On my ranch we have an old horse named Tony, and he is a wonderful horse. He belongs to my niece Mary. When Mary was little, she had yellow braids and a golden, sun-tinted skin. She was not more than two years old before we had her riding horses. Once, behind me on a lively little mare, she shrieked with joy when the mare shied and whirled. "Make him do it again," she demanded.

Every summer vacation Mary came to stay at the ranch and spent most of her time with the animals. At other times she lived with her parents in San Diego. When they bought a house near the city's edge, Mary saw girls and boys her age out riding and she insisted she needed a horse to keep in her own backyard.

None of my ranch horses seemed capable of becoming city horses, so we finally decided to buy a horse for Mary.

He would need to be one that could endure city sights and smells. Also, he had to be stake-broken so that he could be tethered on a long rope or chain and thus be able to enjoy the tall grass that grew on the vacant lots.

I told everyone I knew about the kind of horse we wanted. One day our blacksmith, Tom La Madrid, said, "I think I've found a horse for Mary. He belongs to a fellow Alex knows. The boy has to move away and can't keep him, but he'd like him to go to a good home. Alex trained him. He's a good cowhorse, and he likes to race, too. He's mostly thoroughbred. His father is supposed to be Black Tony and Black Tony is a son of Man of War."

Any horse that Alex Baron had ever trained couldn't help but be a good horse. Alex was of Mexican descent and there were two things he loved to do. One was to sing and the other was to train horses. Mostly he did both at the same time.

I knew that the horse Tom recommended must be a good one and I went to see him at once. He was six years old and, except for one short white sock and a star on his forehead, solid black. He was built as if he were meant to cut the wind. Slim and long-legged, he had the prettiest little head, a long thick mane and tail. He had alert but- tony eyes and small ears that pricked up at whatever thing caught his interest. This was nearly everything that he saw.

Immediately I bought him for Mary. That day I was riding my wise little mare, Cherie, and Cherie and I led Tony home. Ever since then Cherie has been Tony's favor- ite. Being a new horse, he looked upon her as his friend because she had brought him to our ranch.

When Mary came to the ranch and saw Tony for the first time, out in pasture with his friend, she was entranced. She was intrigued by his thoroughbred blood lines, with the feeling that he was a very special horse. She loved his tallness and his build. He was immediately interested, came to her with head high and ears alert to see what she had to offer. He and Cherie had been grazing with quick earnest bites on the short green grass. Cherie, to whom Mary was no stranger, looked up briefly. Tony felt that he had to see about things. This is an attitude he displays to this day.

Mary talked to him, let him put his nose into her cupped hand, tickled his small soft muzzle with her fingers, looked into his eyes.

What she liked best was his chin. It looked exactly like the chin of Man of War in a big framed picture she had. It was a well-rounded, determined chin, not large, but just right for a human hand to feel.

She looked at his long straight legs, his neat hoofs. She felt him with her hands. He put his nose to her hair, sniffed along her face.

We put saddle and bridle on him and Mary rode him for the first time there in the river pasture. He stepped out surely and lightly with his single-footing gait, making a pattern on the sandy trail. She lifted his rein slightly and he galloped with a lightness and a freedom she had never felt before. Mary was swinging with the hills and valleys on the horizon; she felt as if she and Tony were bounding with a rhythm that would go on forever.

His black mane fell back to touch her hand on the rein, his stride over the earth seemed as soft as the feel of his flicking mane.

Since then, Mary and Tony have traveled many miles together. They took trips into the hills for pleasure, and they took journeys between ranch and city home and back again, depending on school and vacation schedules.

Between city and ranch the riding was bad because part of the way was along the sides of paved highways. This is always dangerous for both horse and rider. A horse, startled by some roadside thing, is likely to shy out into the highway and traffic.

But Tony always used extraordinarily good judgment. When darkness overtook them and they had nothing to see but glaring lights, he kept moving briskly. One evening, suddenly startled by the appearance of a cow looming up darkly from a roadside pasture, Tony shied and whirled. But his good sense, even in that moment of panic, kept him from the traffic. He ran. But he ran back toward the way he had come, not stepping once from the highway's shoulder. Mary got him stopped, turned in the desired direction. When he drew near to the spot where he had been terrified, he snorted and trembled but kept stepping forward.

Mary relaxed and thought that here was a horse who could take care of them both. Any other would have shied straight away from the sudden sight of the cow, would have ended in the midst of fast-traveling traffic. It had been Tony's choice, even when he felt he must run for his life, to consider both dangers and run where it was safest.

On another dark night on a trail, Mary suddenly felt herself airborne. In the midst of a long striding gallop, Tony gave a tremendous leap, then kept on running, as soon as he was back on earth. We rode out the next day to see what could have caused his panic. There, plain in the dust, was the track of a big rattlesnake across the trail.

The more we knew Tony the more we came to trust him.

But he was not a solemn animal. Tony always loved fun and excitement. Horse shows and parades made him cavort and dance. If, even from a distance, he heard a loudspeaker or the sound of music, immediately his hoofs seemed inches above earth, his neck arched, his tail flagged up. He gave his rider the feeling that at any moment he might not be underneath the saddle where he belonged.

Yet once entered in any show or a gymkhana, Tony, for all his high spirits, was out to win. Racing was his joy. He could cut the time to the shortest second, spinning around the turn of a course so that the inside stirrup touched the dust as he leaned.

Once at a gymkhana Mary had to race while balancing an egg in a teaspoon. She wisely left problems like speed and jockeying for position up to Tony and concentrated on being able to tilt egg and spoon, bank with Tony's slope around a curving track.

It was the sort of game where speed was not so important as the tender care of the egg. But Tony could run so smoothly that it was best to let him go. Any attempt to slow him would surely have spilled the egg. There would have been a break in the smoothness of his stride and too much joggling for the egg's safety.

Far ahead of any competition, Tony crossed the finish line. Mary led him to collect the blue ribbon and Tony turned his shining eyes and his small quick ears toward her. He might have been saying, "Wasn't that fun!" He liked the applause and stepped proudly as he went away with his ribbon.

Mary and Tony learned from each other. He learned that she would always provide for him, she learned to trust him and feel safe with him, no matter how high his spirits might soar. His attitude was that he enjoyed any time spent with his rider. He wanted to see what would happen next.

During the months in the city each year, Tony adapted to people ways. He lived in a corral and enjoyed the shelter of his own small barn there in a city backyard. He soon knew the pattern of things in winter. He knew that when mornings were still dark a light would always go on in the house. This meant that breakfast would come soon. He would whinny loudly to announce his pleasure. To him a light in the house meant good things, so if the family were away, came home late at night, flashed on a light, Tony began his loud rejoicing.

As days lengthened and spring came on, Tony was tethered to graze on a vacant lot. There he could be left safely all night. Early in the morning Mary put buckets of water and Tony's breakfast in a wheelbarrow and trundled it to him. Immediately Tony associated a wheelbarrow with all good things and anything that looked like one interested him.

Therefore he deduced that a baby carriage probably contained something good. Tony, being ridden sedately down a street, would see a baby carriage, rush to peer and sniff at the infant inside it, while its mother was being scared half out of her wits. Since the baby was neither edible nor interesting, Tony promptly moved on. Mary learned to take a tight rein whenever a pushed vehicle appeared on a sidewalk.

Not always in the city did Tony get enough exercise. Mary found a way to play with him when she didn't have time to ride. She rolled a tire across his corral. He stared and snorted as it turned, wobbled, stopped and fell over. She rolled it again and he chased it, struck at it with a

front hoof. It was a puppy-like thing to do, not horse-like at all. Tony's nostrils flared, eyes shining wildly, ears alert. He loved this game.

One winter there came rains enough so that creeks roared and there were bogs in unexpected places. After heavy rains these bogs are invisible. The terrain looks the same everywhere; then suddenly a rider finds a floundering, frightened horse beneath him, a horse that keeps trying to move forward, lunging violently to reach firm earth.

After one such experience, Tony would not endure another. The odd thing about these bogs is that they are not necessarily in low places. A low spot with standing water is almost sure not to be a bog. But you can suddenly feel your horse go down on an innocent-looking grassy slope. A few horses knew all about this, and Tony was one of them. If, suddenly, when traveling briskly along, he stopped and put his nose to the earth it was time to let him make his choice about the direction of his next few steps. Only if he were urged and prodded against his will would he step even near what he knew to be unsafe footing. It must have been that his sense of smell informed him that underneath the grass there was too much moisture. He had his own ideas about what was best to do or not to do. It was always wiser to trust his horse sense.

The winter of the many rains was one when my horses had to wade creeks and leap over smaller rivulets. Almost always Tony went willingly through or over any waterway. But late one day when he had traveled far and was coming home in a roundabout way, he and Mary came to a swift stream, deep within the banks it had cut. He didn't like it. Mary searched for a crossing upstream, downstream, found no easy-looking place for fording. She had circled so far that this *had* to be the way home, for soon it would be dark.

Tony said no. Mary said yes. Tony rebelled, kept whirling away from the roaring water.

"We've got to," Mary told him.

Tony expressed his opinion that the stream was too wide, too swift, too deep. Mary kept urging him, kept insisting, gave him a few good whacks.

Tony indicated that if he had to cross he would, but that it was an unsafe thing to try. He gathered himself and leaped mightily. He hadn't thought he could make it and he almost didn't. His front hoofs barely touched the further bank and it fell away with a turbulence of sand and rushing water. Tony's haunches sank back, but only to give him the second start he needed. Another leap and his front hoofs found slightly firmer footing, so that with the power of his front legs he managed to pull out. His heart pounded from the effort and his breath came with sobbing, rasping sounds. But he turned bright eyes to Mary as she slipped off and started leading him slowly along to let him get his wind back.

Mary's respect for Tony's judgment must have been greater than his for hers. Tony was always right—and he knew it.

But the best part of Tony isn't what he did under saddle, or in times of stress. It is Tony himself, courageous when necessary, ridiculous at times, playful and strong of personality.

Mary and I don't like to kill rattlesnakes or anything else, but if a rattlesnake is near barn or home pastures we feel we have to kill it because of dogs, cats and livestock. One day we showed Tony a dead rattlesnake. Immediately his ears shot up, his neck arched, his eyes blazed, and two front hoofs struck out at the snake held toward him on a stick. Then he became almost morbidly entranced by it and did not want us to go away with it. He kept circling, pawing, snorting. We put it down on the earth and he drew near, with his four feet braced, ready for a sudden backward leap. He stretched his head forward, his nose went within cautious distance of the snake, his breathing became so intense that we could see his sides moving. He jumped away, then carefully moved back toward the snake to let his nostrils get thrillingly close. He was horrifying himself and seeming to enjoy it. His sense of the dramatic has always been great.

Tony always came near to watch any horse that needed care from the veterinary. If another horse's teeth were being fixed, Tony loved to come and peer, as if he were getting some dreadful type of satisfaction from the whole operation.

Once we saw him do the oddest thing we ever saw any horse do and we haven't any idea why he did it. Mary and I were riding along a dirt road when Tony spotted an ordinary-looking stick lying in the dust. He pulled his head toward it and Mary let him reach down and sniff. He sniffed so intently that we saw his sides moving like bellows. With his nose against the stick, he pivoted his back quarters in a circle, continuing to take in interested breaths. His eyes bulged, his ears were at the highest point of attention.

We dismounted to examine the stick ourselves, to try to find something unusual about it. We discovered nothing and put it down. Tony continued to be entranced. He shoved the stick with his nose. Probably he would have stayed there for hours, but we wanted to move on, and Tony moved away reluctantly. I don't know why we didn't take the stick home for his further enjoyment. No one ever knew why Tony behaved in such a way.

Now it is years since Tony has been ridden. He is so old that his black face is frosted. So much of it is white with age that we can scarcely find the star that once shone so brightly on his forehead.

Some mornings when I let him out of his stall after his breakfast it seems that he can scarcely hobble. He moves with the burden of years heavy upon him.

Then comes a springlike morning, the kind that can come before April, before it is really spring. There is something in the earth, something in the smell of the air. There is some great and wonderful message which Tony receives and takes unto himself.

He, the ancient gelding, suddenly considers himself to be a splendid young stallion. He sends forth a wild whinny that beats against a hill and echoes back. He starts off, trotting stiffly as an old horse does. Then he breaks into his old swinging gallop. He has forgotten his rheumatism. His nostrils have expanded, his eyes have brightened, his ears have come alive.

He gallops across the short green grass and causes all the mares to come in season. They nearly swoon in admiration. They quarrel among themselves over Tony's attentions. He parades, struts, arches his neck.

Often he has a mock battle with Attu, nearly as old as himself. The two geldings rear to strike at one another, bite at knees, drop gracefully on one front leg, rise to whirl and swing playful kicks. The mares whinny, run in circles, stop to stare excitedly.

Finally, every one grows tired, Tony lies down on the sun-warmed grass of just-before-spring. He rests, sprawled out as a young colt sprawls, breathing quickly, with the sun hot upon his coat.

We hope that many more such days will come before, sometime, Tony sleeps and forgets about waking up.

THREE COLTS

One summer day I was watching my three colts, Don Ramon, Cherokee and Little Larry, and I was thinking how the world must seem to them. If you were a colt, I reflected, this earth must be a perfect place. It might not be so good if you were a king or a congressman or a dictator or an office worker. People in tenement houses in big cities probably find little to their liking in summer. And people with what is known as World Affairs on their minds surely find little to their liking at any time.

But the colts knew that the earth was good. On this particular very warm day these three were sprawled out under an oak tree, their mothers standing drowsily near, and I thought how very much I'd like to round up all the troublesome, quarrelsome leaders of people in order to let them see how easy and attractive life can be. But I concluded that it wouldn't be of much use. None of them would think that colts were very important, and just because life was good in a summer pasture didn't mean that life would be good everywhere.

But my colts thought that it was. Even Little Larry, who was fragile, was glad to be alive. He said so when he cavorted across the pastures with his sturdier brothers, trotting high, with action prettier than theirs, rearing and whirling, graceful as a little dream foal.

Someone suggested that I should have named him Angel, because soon he might be one. But when he was born, when I first saw him standing on his straight little legs, I had no inkling that all might not be well with Larry. I was so happy for his mother, Betty, that he was born. Betty was a golden-brown buckskin with a thick mane and tail and big shining dark eyes, and I'd often thought that she must be the bravest mare in the world.

A long time ago, when she had another colt with her, she broke her knee when she was miles from home, grazing in the hills. She came home with the colt because she needed help. She came dragging along on three legs, up steep rocky trails, over the ridge, down the rough stony trail. It must have taken her several days to get there. She was very gaunt from thirst and hunger and pain.

We sent her to the large animal hospital, where she stayed in a cast until it was discovered that sores were developing under the cast, and that the cast did no good anyway. Her knee tightened up, in time, so she could hobble around, but she was badly crippled. The vet said he had never seen such a brave mare. We thought that her colts might inherit her courage and stamina.

And Little Larry did. Otherwise I think he might not have lived long at all.

He was the prettiest of the colts, very delicate. He was pale gold color, a pinkish gold, and his friends, who often inquired about him, called him the pink pony. Children loved him. His eyes were big and dark, his ears small, well shaped, and his face was like the face of an Arabian. His mane and tail were red and white, adding to his look of pinkness.

At first I thought it was because his mother was letting down milk too fast that milk came pouring out of his nose. Finally the vet saw him, said he had a split palate and would never get enough to eat because, always, food would drop out of his nose. It was evident that Little Larry was underfed, and the vet thought an immediate operation was necessary. He picked him up, put him in his car, took him to the hospital and operated, while his mother, left at home, worried all day.

That night I went after him to bring him home and I sat on the back seat of the car and stood Larry on the floor where I could steady him. He didn't like it there. He climbed up on my lap and went to sleep and didn't waken until we reached our own front gate. Somehow he knew he was home and began to whinny. By the beam of a flashlight we watched him nurse his mother—and not a drop of milk came out of his nose.

I didn't dare to be too happy about this because the vet had said that it was likely the stitches wouldn't hold. He really hadn't much faith in the operation. He was right.

Soon Little Larry was wasting as much milk as ever.

People said he ought to be killed, and I thought perhaps it would be kinder. But slowly he was growing and, there was no doubt about it, he was a happy colt. I watched him playing, shying at shadows and leaves, pretending he had to buck mountain lions off his back, jumping away from rattlesnakes. I watched him tire a little sooner than the other colts, then sprawl out on the warm earth to sleep. In spite of everything, he was having a good time and his mother was happy to own him. Being a young colt is an exquisite adventure, and I couldn't deprive this one of his life. I began feeding him calf manna and, though he lost much of it through his always gummy little nose, he got enough of it to help.

The vet said that if he lived to grow bigger, a second operation would be easier to perform and less dangerous. Perhaps it might even be successful. So there was nothing for Larry to do but wait, grow as much as he could, play when he felt like it, and try to get all the milk, water, calf manna and grass possible past the slit way back there in the roof of his mouth. Larry didn't know that anything was wrong. He thought that this was the way life was and he went about making the best of it. He had caught the knack of living.

His tough little half-brothers reared up to spar with each other, like fighting stallions, striking out with front hoofs. They tore at each other's throats. Larry watched, then reached instinctively for the spot where, if he chose, he could hamstring one of them. There was a tangle of three colts going around and around, until one broke away and started a race. Their mothers, who all worried over their first foals, were now wise old brood mares and let the colts play together.

So there was their world. Sunshine and shade. Leaves and dry grass to sample. Mother mares to love them, big geldings to tag admiringly after. They had one another to play with. They beat the earth with their hoofs. They got down and rolled upon it, they stretched out and slept, absorbing its strength. It belonged to them and it served them well.

PIG

Two baby goats used to like to wander down to the pasture of our stallion, Don Roscoe, and at first it worried me, for they were very small. But the stallion knew they were small and he was careful not to step on them. He liked them and would put down his head and touch them gently.

Later, when they were big goats, but still playful, they had fun with the colts, racing and rearing up to bunt. The colts, too, would rear and wave their hoofs at the goats. One little filly, Rosalys, actually learned how to play like a goat and when the goat would rear up and push against her forehead, she would push back. It was a very uncoltlike way to play and amazed people who watched her.

It charms me when animals of different kinds make friends with one another. But no combination has ever struck me so funny as that of my horses and Pig.

I don't know where Pig came from. One morning when I took some horses to drink at a well a mile from the barn, there was Pig, rooting under an oak tree. As soon as she saw us she made a sound that was half whistle, half squeal, and raced across the clearing to hide in the brush. The horses were as astonished as I. They felt very nervous about Pig's appearance, and, smelling Pig, did a deal of snorting before they'd take their morning drink.

After that, we saw the half-grown red and white pig every time we went to the well. For a long time we didn't have a good look at her because she was in such a hurry to run and hide.

But gradually she grew used to the horses and they to her. After awhile she followed the horses home. I thought she might take up with cows, sheep and goats, who, being cloven-hoofed, were more her kind. But Pig liked only horses.

The horses didn't particularly like her. But there she was, always literally underfoot, and, except at feeding time, they didn't mind. When I fed the mare Betty and her colt Little Larry their grain, Pig was right there, with both front hoofs in the feed pan. They'd strike, bite, kick. Pig would scream bloody murder but go right on gobbling the grain as fast as ever she could.

When she went for another mare's grain, the mare, Cherie, jumped up and down with rage. All the time she was trying to eat she kept jumping up and down.

Don Roscoe, on his hind legs, waving murderous front hoofs, routed Pig in a hurry. Pig screamed wild protests

but scooted under the fence. That was at first; Pig was more determined than any horse. She kept returning until Don Roscoe grew tired of chasing her out. One day I saw him bend down and nibble her ears gently, and the next day I saw him sharing his hay with her. And when I rode him down the road for the mail one evening, Pig came trotting after. After that I had difficulty persuading her to stay home. I didn't want her going out on the highway.

But it was Little Larry and Betty that Pig liked best. The reason might have been that the colt kept spilling food and Pig disliked missing any source of nourishment. Little Larry actually enjoyed Pig and spent time scratching her back by nibbling up and down her spine. Once in awhile, though, he bit too hard and Pig shrieked. One time I heard her screaming as if her throat were being slit. When I rushed to see, Little Larry was merely standing quietly, holding one of Pig's ears between his teeth.

Pig had no respect for horse hoofs, in spite of many kicks. She walked under horses; if a hoof was in her way she bit an ankle. For this she was kicked, which caused much shrieking, but the next ankle in her way got bitten just the same. At night, when a horse stood dozing, Pig liked to lie down underneath—and was furious when her warm roof walked off from over her. When a horse was lying down, Pig lay with her body pressed against his, nice and warm.

The horses, with the exception, perhaps, of Little Larry, had no affection at all for Pig, and, whenever they could, went off to graze without her. This put Pig to a lot of trouble as she had to go and find them. She would trot along, grumbling to herself, squealing indignantly.

She simply could not bear it if I put a horse in the barn for a feed of grain and she couldn't get in to get some. She would fly into a perfect rage and scream at the top of her voice. One time she was so mad that she grabbed an old pair of blue jeans the dogs had been playing with and tore them to shreds, eying me wickedly.

Once she made me mount a colt before I felt the colt was ready. I don't like to mount a colt so quickly that it is startled. I like to put weight in the stirrup, letting the young animal get used to things gradually. This time, just as I put a foot in the stirrup and waited a minute to see if the colt were going to take alarm, Pig came and bit my ankle. I flung myself into the saddle. This scared the colt, who took off with a leap, and I was sure that for some time after that he would be frightened about being mounted.

In a way, I suppose knowing Pig was good training for the colts. At least they never took fright at any other pig they saw.

TRIPPIT'S COLT

I went to my friend Mardy's ranch to see Trippit's new colt. Mardy wasn't around, she was somewhere at the other end of the ranch, so I walked out into Trippit's pasture. Trippit was an Arabian-looking gray mare and her little colt, who was going to be gray, was black, as most gray colts are at birth. I stared at him and laughed, for I had never seen such a little goblin, such a little imp. Just what there was about him that seemed so extraordinary would be hard to explain. He looked like many another—small of body, long of legs. He had that wise bulge at the forehead that the new foal wears for awhile; the bulge is, I think, to protect its head at birth. Maybe it was his eyes that pleased me so, the way he rolled them and showed the whites. You felt the strength of his personality.

I sat in the grass and he came to touch me with his nose. His mother, who had kept nickering to him and had wanted to keep her body between him and me, finally relaxed and decided I was trustworthy. Some colts are bashful when they are tiny, but this little one had a great curiosity. He wanted to taste me and he pawed at me with a tiny front hoof. Then he turned, gave a little flirt of tail and hind hoofs, but didn't kick. Instead, he walked solemnly away, stumbled, and immediately had to duck his head and kick up his heels. Every little colt I ever knew will do this. If he accidentally stumbles he has to give a frolic to pretend he really wasn't stumbling, he did it on purpose, he was playing.

Trippit spoke to him anxiously and hurried to see if he was all right. This insult to his dignity made him put his ears flat back and glare at his mother crossly. *He* didn't need any mama watching over him every minute.

Little colts always look astonished. And the way the short frizzly mane stood up on this one added to his look of surprise. Trippit, too, had a look about her, as if she knew that all this joy that had come to her was a miracle of unending wonder.

Trippit was one who had always longed for a colt. Each spring when Dinah, Mardy's bay mare, had hers, Trippit grew so passionate that she would even chase after people, nickering lovingly. Mardy actually used to have to run from her own mare, laughing as she ran, for Trippit was feeling so in love with the world and so demonstrative that she'd knock her down with joy and start nuzzling her and talking to her as if she were a colt.

None of us had ever seen a mare so filled with maternal instinct as Trippit was. The year before this, she had had a tragedy, losing her unborn foal. She had tried hard to bring the little immature thing to life, licking it and speaking to it, and for days afterwards she grieved.

Now she had this new one, so lively, so sure of its place on earth. In her gray face Trippit's eyes always looked big and dark. Now, as she watched her colt, those eyes seemed bigger than ever. And she was always watching it, every move it made, and nickering to it. And she trembled with delight when it answered her, with a sound half squeal, half nicker.

Trippit's udder had been full and uncomfortably tight when the foal was born, and when first he started to nurse she had squealed and drawn up her belly, muscles tense with pain. But even the pain seemed to please her. She had stood still, only turning her head to touch the sweet little rump. Mares, even experienced brood mares, are likely to step around and complain a little at the hurt of the first nursing.

Trippit felt so intense about this colt that sometimes when she just stood staring at him she'd be so filled with maternal emotions that the milk would come spurting from her. He was so young this first time I saw him that he was lean, but I knew that in a day or so Trippit would have him looking round and bouncy.

Already he felt bouncy, looking for excuses to jump, pretending things about trees and shadows. He felt very secure, for he knew his mother would never let anything happen to him. He was so little he could walk back and forth under her belly to get flies off his back. As I watched, he deviated and came walking out from between her hind legs. Everything he did was amusing. He would roll his eyes at me after every antic as if to make sure he had an appreciative audience.

The way he arched his neck, the extreme fineness of his head and the smallness of his muzzle reminded me of a sea horse. I wondered what Mardy would name him. It would be difficult to find a name that exactly fitted such a one.

As it turned out, he never had a name. Later, we spoke of him as Trippit's little nameless one.

A few nights after he died I was again at Mardy's. It was a warm night, of moonlight and shadows, and all evening Trippit kept walking through shadow and light, like a ghost herself, searching for her little colt. She would go far off, and from far off we could hear her whinny, then her galloping hoofs sounded nearer as she returned to look in the grassy spot where he had been born. Oddly, it was to the spot of foaling that she kept returning, not to the oak under which he had died.

I never remember a sadder evening. The poor-wills mourned and the kill-deer had no cheery sound. Even the breeze sounded sad and listless in oak leaves.

Later we said to each other, "Who knows? Maybe Trippit's little one has saved the lives of other colts." But it was a hard way to find comfort.

The colt had died of a navel infection. Because of him we are careful to put antiseptic on the navel of each new foal.

ATTU

Attu's father was a fiery red Arabian named Fernas. His mother was a small black and white pony. Though his mother was a pony, Attu grew to normal horse size. From her he inherited a thick mane and shining buttony eyes. In color he turned out to be the soft brown of a deer. From his father he had an Arabian look, with the high proud tail carriage of an Arabian. He arched his neck and stepped proudly.

My friend Margo gave him to me when he was four years old. He was shining and fat and excited the day a horse trailer brought him to me.

He had been schooled a little by a horse trainer, but when I got on him to ride for the first time, it was as though he were trying to go in six different directions at once. He had no idea of how to rein. He was not disturbed at having saddle and rider on him, or a bit in his mouth; he simply didn't know what to do about anything. I was delighted with him and not worried about his ignorance. I knew that soon he would learn all he needed to know.

Until he knew more about his new home he would need to live in a safe corral. He was accustomed to a small corral in his city home. He was also accustomed to seeing familiar horses, and he was fond of Margo. He had known her forever, as far as he was concerned, as she had been present at his birth.

Now, in a new place, with no familiar horse or human around, Attu was immediately homesick. All the horses that came to look over his fence were strangers. He paced up and down and whinnied and whinnied.

If I stayed with him to pet him and talk, all was well. The minute I left, his despairing voice echoed back from the hills. He paced like a caged coyote and lamented. Hay and grain were no solace. In a week he was thin, bony and haggard. I was terrified lest Margo come to visit him, for she was sure to think I was starving him.

Thin as he was, I decided it would be good to ride him a little every day and teach him to rein. At least, if I were riding him, he would not be alone. And out in my pastures he could see the other horses, grow accustomed to them.

When I got on him he traveled willingly enough along a level trail, though he whinnied loudly as he walked. I began to admire his ears, which were very tiny above mane and forelock. They were upright, possibly in anticipation of meeting a horse he knew.

We came to a dry creek bed where the trail had to dip down and up to cross it. Attu had never been ridden in hill country. The terrain he knew was flat and he did not believe that under his hoofs earth could go up and down. He stood firmly on four hoofs and stared into the wide shallow dip. Though there was a good worn trail dipping down and going up, he resolved that this was no safe place for travel.

I urged. He kept whirling with intent to hurry away. Again and again I turned him back demandingly. Finally I felt him gathering himself. From a standstill he gave such a mighty leap that for a moment I thought we would land on a distant hilltop. But he didn't quite make it across. He landed just short of the far bank and didn't know what to do. The spot where he stood in the sandy bed was level enough, but there was no way for him to go anywhere but up and out. This he seemed to consider. I urged him nowhere. I felt that it was up to him to decide how to return to the kind of level going he liked. I was positive that he would not stand there forever.

He looked around and whinnied. He looked up the bank, he put his nose to the side of the bank. Again I felt him call on his muscles. Again he took to the air. This time, somehow, he managed to leap from the creek bed to the top. He made a neat landing. Then joyfully he kicked up his heels and, after that, he broke into a swinging gallop. He was pleased with himself. His gallop was a purely Arabian gait, effortless and easy. I let him circle and headed him toward home and his lonely corral.

The next time we rode to the same place he walked down sedately, then galloped up the trail and out. Ever afterwards, when we followed a trail that dipped down and up, Attu galloped up. This is a thing that most horses like to do, but Attu was more intense about it. Always he wanted to run up any steep place. I, enjoying his action, never tried to check him.

Most horses like other horses better than people, but Attu had the Arabian characteristic of being fond of people. Even after he was turned out to graze with the others, he was glad to see a human approach. He was the only horse I ever had that would actually reach out to seize a bit.

Once he recovered from his homesickness, he put on weight and began to look respectable again. He was still of the opinion that a human is the best friend a horse can have. His attitude was flattering, of course. It may have been caused by the fact that his first owner was understanding and loving toward horses.

But in spite of his interest in people, whenever I put a bucket of grain before him he'd swing and kick at me. One time he gave me a good kick which sent me through the air for some feet, and it hurt. Margo said she thought the reason for this behavior was that when he lived in his corral in the city, he had been teased by children passing by. Probably they had offered him a handful of grass and had then snatched it away.

At any rate, for years the first thing Attu did at feeding time was to start to kick. One day the stallion Don Roscoe got loose, chased Attu and chewed him up around the base of his tail. The wounds had to have medication. Oddly enough, at this time I could give him hay and grain to keep him standing quietly and could then doctor his poor tail. I pressed myself closely against his back legs so that in case he did kick he would not have a powerful swing. But he simply stood, enjoying his food and paying no attention to what was going on back there.

After that, he did not kick at me so much but he continued to make an uproar about any cow, horse, pig or dog that approached at feeding time. Our pet pigs soon learned not to plan to make Attu share his feed with them. To this day, as he kicks he manages to roar like a lion and at the same time shriek as loudly as do the pigs.

Whenever I rode Attu far back into the hills and stopped for lunch I turned him free. Any other horse would have headed for home. But Attu had such a phobia about being alone that he wouldn't leave even a human being. He walked around and grazed, but kept an eye on me. If I started investigating a deer trail that went off through the brush, the next thing I knew Attu was right behind me, treading on my heels. The only time I ever tied him and walked away he was frantic, whinnying at the top of his voice, pulling at his rope. If I were on an overnight trip and sleeping on the ground, I was sure that if Attu were turned free he would still be near in the morning. He was the only horse I ever knew who had this dog-like need of companionship, for a horse is a herd animal and usually prefers to be with others of his own kind.

This trait of his was sometimes very helpful. Once we had a big pet steer that was greatly given to wandering. One day Attu and I found him far away, off down a steep brushy hill. If I left the steer he would wander down to the cattle ranch in the valley below and we'd have a very bad time getting him home. We had to get him at once.

I tried driving him, but it was useless. He didn't want to go up the steep trail and so he plunged into dense thickets where I could not ride after him. Finally, I got off Attu, attached my rope to the steer, got back on the horse and tried to lead the steer. He would lead well if I led him on foot, but he had respect for the rear end of Attu and he would not come behind him. I gave my rope a turn around the saddle horn and Attu pulled as best he could, but the steer was stronger than we were. He kept plunging from side to side, trying to escape into the brush. I looked at the trail ahead of us, a trail that climbed straight up. Attu and I could never get the steer home in this fashion. Gravity, as well as the steer's intentions, were against us.

I dismounted, tied the steer to a manzanita, all red trunked and beautiful, then placed Attu behind the steer, put his reins up over the saddle horn. I untied the steer and started leading him along the narrow brushy trail. Attu marched behind him, and when the steer demonstrated that he didn't want to go any further up the hill, Attu reached out and bit him. I kept climbing, the steer kept coming, Attu kept seeing to it that he did. It took us hours to get home, but it was worth it. None of my other horses would have helped me in this way.

For many years Attu and I enjoyed one another. Attu's charm was that he was fun to ride alone; if he had any human up top he was not lonely for another horse. Every spring he shed so shining brown he was almost a mirror, and he felt so lively that the first few steps of a gallop also meant some cavorting. Attu was one of the few horses I owned that never tossed me off. His playfulness was an undulating, joyful thing to ride.

As years went on Attu became blind in one eye. The eye stayed bright and shining, but he couldn't see out of it. When I rode him I had to be careful about his right side, watch out for rocks and brush.

I couldn't let him go out to graze in hilly rough pastures, he had no seeing-eye horse as Penny once had. So he lived in the home pasture, close to house and barn, which pleased him because he saw people every day. It was handy for me to have such a horse near, as Attu always came when I called him, and if I needed to hurry after some straying cow I could depend on him.

One time in early summer I was riding him with a group of others and Attu was feeling extra-lively. We were all galloping through a small green swale when he suddenly seemed overcome with joy. He cavorted, missed seeing a rock on his right side, and fell. Neither he nor I were in the least hurt. Attu scrambled to his feet and hurried to catch up with the others.

But I thought that it had been stupid of me to let him risk injury; he could have broken a leg. It had been an extra-good ride, but the same thing could happen to Attu again.

Anyway, by now he was old, even if he didn't know it. A horse that receives good care can last a long time, and Attu is lasting. He hasn't been ridden since that summer day, but he has a good time with his horse friends and his human friends. Every spring he and old Tony remember what fun it was to be colts, and together they race across the grass.

LYNETTE

A newborn human isn't aware of anything for a long time. When finally it does realize it is alive and begins to look around, it is somewhat accustomed to the idea of living and isn't so very surprised. Puppies, kittens, rats and all other things that are born helpless lose the fun of suddenly finding themselves alive and able to move about. Their awareness of life comes gradually.

But creatures like calves and colts and pigs and lambs, babies that must stand on their own feet and walk almost immediately, have an air of astonishment and delight. The first warm drink of milk puts such strength into lambs that they begin to caper at once, and little kids begin being little goats right away. The milk sometimes makes colts and calves so sleepy they must postpone play until after their first nap, but soon they try to make their hoofs express their joy of living. The first few hours of life are especially magic ones, for they are wholly free of fear. Soon enough the young learn that this is a dangerous world, but Nature, for once letting kindness interfere with wisdom, gives them the great gift of experiencing complete security. For a brief time they are allowed to feel that all the universe has kindly intentions. During this magic interval the new foal will approach you on trembling legs and put its nose to your face. The lamb will follow you if you move and the little goat will press its forehead hard against the palm of your hand. For that time the earth is as harmless as it is lovely, the earth seems as young and sweet as the newborn, and the imaginative human mind is given a glimpse into the realm of heaven.

Then is the time to caress the warm soft young, to get them accustomed to your nearness. At any moment the first expression of fear will come, the dreadful awareness that all may not be well. By the next day, unless you have fondled them a great deal, the young will run from you.

When I walked through the rain-wet grass to see the new foal, its mother, the mare Cherie, looked as if I should not come so near, and put herself between her child and me. But after I had petted the mother and talked to her softly she let the foal come toward me and I touched its soft little head and felt its warm breath.

This foal was a filly, very tall and straight legged, as sturdy a new one as I had ever seen. Her body was very light brown, almost gold, and her kinky mane and tail were black. Like her mother, she had a star on her forehead, and a snip of white toward her nostrils.

It had rained hard all night and was going to rain some more, but the little filly was convinced that life was wonderful. She wanted to walk around and look at things, she wanted to nurse her mother, she wanted to lie down in the grass and rest. She wanted to try running a little, but this worried her mother, who chased after her with anxious nickerings.

When the other horses came crowding around the fence to watch, the mare was furious. She got between them and the foal and somehow curved her body in a rigid attempt at enfolding her child, then turned her head to glare at them. A sharp whistling breath of anger came from her flared nostrils and her eyes were red. Her pose showed nothing of the softness of the mother love that prompted it; she was hard with anger.

The foal, still deep in its dream of loveliness, saw no reason for this and wanted to go look at the interested ones. Her own father was neighing wildly, prancing back and forth along his fence, angry at the others for being near.

He had no wish to harm his little daughter, he wanted only to see her clearly, and he would like to have touched her with his nose. But Cherie took her foal back among the bushes where neither he nor any of the others could see her at all.

For a few days there was no gentle weather—the wind was not tempered to the new foal. I wanted to get it into a warm dry stall. First I had to corral all other horses and I shut the stallion in a box stall. When I started leading

Cherie, with the little one following, such an uproar started that Cherie grew frantic. The foal's father looked over his stall door and threatened to jump out; and Cherie had no wish to be shut in a barn so near him. If I did get her in a stall I felt she would try to kick it down, for when I let the others loose I knew they would crowd around to look in.

All this excitement delighted the little filly, so she kept scampering away from her mother, thus making her all the wilder. It seemed simpler to put them back in the wet pasture, which they didn't seem to mind anyway. For the first days of its life the foal couldn't have known what comfort meant, but it seemed perfectly satisfied with an existence that was always cold and wet. It thought this was the way life was, and it enjoyed playing and sleeping in the wet grass and nursing its mother and looking at things.

I kept thinking what a perfectly wonderful surprise the foal was going to have when it felt warm sunshine for the first time. If, under dark wet skies, it thought that life was delightful, whatever would it do when the sun shone bright?

The first sunny day of the foal's life was one of those very sweet, soft days when lilacs make the air smell like honey and the birds sing the certain songs they sing only in March and April. After days of rain, Lynette, as we finally named the little filly, was suddenly to find that she didn't have to work at keeping warm. With no effort on her part, she could be comfortable. She didn't have to press close to her mother's wet side, hunting for warmth.

Her mother was so glad about the change in the weather that she stretched out flat and took a sunbath. Lynette lay down too, a golden-brown blob on the green grass. But after awhile she must have started to dream about her mother for she whinnied in her sleep. She woke up and scrambled to her feet and looked to Cherie for a drink.

Cherie regarded her with one sleepy eye and remained prone. Lynette wandered all around her, poking with a hungry nose, but Cherie sighed deeply and would not move. Lynette whickered at her and pawed with a tiny front hoof. This, I thought, was exactly how some poor little colt would act if its mother were sick and couldn't stand up. This was how Cherie herself had behaved when her own mother lay dying, before she came to my ranch to be fed on a nursing bottle. Under different circumstances this could be a sad sight, but now I could enjoy it, for all was well.

Cherie whinnied softly, as if telling Lynette to lie down and go to sleep because mama wanted to rest a while longer. But the voice of her mother only made the foal more eager to be fed, and she kept trying to prod Cherie to her feet. Finally, Cherie lifted her head, tucked her front legs under her, and watched Lynette from this more elevated position. This aroused all the little one's hopes; she lipped at her mama's ears and poked at her chin.

At last Cherie uttered a deep whinny and got up and Lynette suckled with noisy pleasure. After all, this was to be her day, her very first day of warm sunshine, and she would enjoy all of it.

Today the two could be put in a larger pasture. When they were, Cherie began at once to pull at the grass, and little Lynette, without a tooth in her head, wanted to graze too. She found that this was not so easy. Though the grass was thick it was not tall, and Lynette's long legs soon caused her to feel that the grass was much too far away. In order to get her nose into it, she had to bend her neck straight down, and then, to bring earth nearer, she had to spraddle out her front legs. Obviously, it hardly seemed worth the effort to get a few wisps of grass, which she couldn't chew properly anyway. She gave up presently and ran in merry little circles around her mother. Then she found a spot of warm damp sand—and was entranced.

She pawed at the sand with one sharp little front hoof, then with the other. The sand flew delightfully. She let herself down into it and then, just like a grown horse, all sweaty from being ridden, she rolled. Her legs waved in the air like the legs of an upside-down bug. She rubbed her back into the sand, flopped over on one side, flopped back to the other—and, with the swiftness with which she did everything, dropped off to sleep. She slept intensely, breathing fast, the sun hot upon her.

By afternoon she had mastered the grazing problem. Instead of standing on her four legs and reaching down to the grass, she stretched flat on her side. With one eye on the sky and the other among grass stems, she stretched out her nose and plucked the grass, gumming away on it until she went to sleep, green wisps sticking out of her mouth.

By early evening she seemed to have decided never to

sleep again. She sprang straight up in the air, exactly as a lamb does, she raced in circles while Cherie whinnied worriedly, she became a bucking bronco and a wild horse —perhaps she even wanted to be Pegasus. Her hoofs, yearning for sky, made a loud sound on the earth.

While Cherie was busy eating her evening pan of grain, the yellow kitten strolled into the pasture. With the boldness of curiosity, the foal stalked the cat, and when he lay down she nosed him gently, fascinated by his scent and the feel of thick, tickly fur against her nose.

The new foal was giant-sized compared with the kitten. One quick, hard paw with a front hoof could hurt him badly, but he knew very well that no such thing would happen. He rolled over on his back, reached up and tapped Lynette's nose with sheathed paws. Lynette backed

up two steps and stared, uncertain, then touched him again and felt the gentle paws on her chin. She rippled his fur with her quick breaths.

Cherie finished her grain, stared, decided that cats were deadly, and rushed excitedly toward her child. The kitten made off, but Lynette was so exhilarated that she ran, bucking and snorting and shying, all around the pasture.

What a lovely, lovely day! In the early starlight I found the foal deep asleep, her mother standing over her drowsily. I knelt and put my face against her and she smelled of sunshine and grass and flowers and sweet warm life.

DOMINGO

The old gray mare would have been surprised to know that I would even consider anything like Domingo as an inheritance from her. But then, so many wonderful things have come to me because I knew her first.

Domingo came when I needed him. At the time I did not realize this, though I knew that he needed me.

It is not my nature to be sad, but I was feeling sorrowful for a number of reasons. I was grieving over some tragedies, both animal and human. Furthermore, it was the bad time of year. In the hills deer were being chased by people with guns, many wounded deer escaped to die slowly. Even worse things were happening. Steel traps were out, coyotes, bobcats, foxes, raccoons were suffering under the hot sun, under the cold stars. This was a strange time of year, just before the rainy season. Mornings were frosty, midday sun burned intensely.

To see Domingo, you would not think that he could help. He arrived unexpectedly.

One November day I was late doing the afternoon chores. It was dark as I finished feeding the cows and horses, carrying water to calves and their mothers. It was the wrong time of year for calves, but three had been born when I hadn't expected them. They were happy little calves, lively and playful. They should have cheered me.

A pickup truck drove into the corral. Three young fellows jumped out. "Look what we've brought you!" one shouted.

I looked in the truckbed. All trussed up on the floor lay a small white burro.

The boys untied him, slid him out—and there stood the thinnest, saddest animal I have ever seen. He was a skeleton on four hoofs.

Already I had more animals of different kinds than anyone in his right mind would have. But what, I thought dimly, is one's right mind?

We led the burro into a stall and I turned on the barn lights. The animal's backbone was at least three inches above the rest of him. His flanks were so caved in that a finger poked on one side could feel a finger poked on the other. His ribs were big ridges, his chest scarcely existed. His rump was almost pure bones, his tail was like the tail of a camel.

I looked at him and he put up his long ears and looked back at me. His ears impressed me, but his eyes impressed me more. They were bright, young, hopeful.

Perhaps, I thought, it is because he is a white burro that his eyes look so big and bright. But it was as if his eyes said he was now a poverty-stricken, under-privileged creature but he hoped that things would be better soon. He was of a breed accustomed to endure.

He had not liked being tied down in a truck. He had banged himself and fought so that his knees, hocks, hip bones and forehead were raw.

I dabbed medicine on his bloody spots while his joyful rescuers tossed him hay. Immediately he began eating.

At last one of the boys explained. "The guy that had him says there is something wrong with him. He didn't want him, so we took him and brought him here to you."

I said, "I don't need him."

"He needs you," the boy said.

I remarked that probably what was wrong with the burro was that he was sick of not eating. We gave him a bucket of water and a bucket with bran in it. He was so weak that he fell down as he was eating. I wondered if he would live through the night.

But the next morning, which was Sunday, I heard a joyful sound as the sun came up over the hill. It was a strange, loud greeting to the sun and the new day. It began with a wheezing rusty sound and ended with blasts of gladness. It was like a prayer of thankfulness. Here was the new day, here was a live burro.

When I went to the barn I called, "Domingo?"

The burro answered by opening his mouth wide. His song began with all the notes that an old-fashioned pump gives out when you are working the handle up and down.

After he had inhaled enough air, he really gave forth. He moaned, groaned, trilled, said "Oh, oh, oh," found two musical notes, made some chords, sobbed, hiccoughed, seemed to growl, ended with more blasts and snorts.

Domingo means Sunday in Spanish. The burro loved the sun, he loved the day. He had named himself.

For weeks I kept Domingo inside the barn. I wanted him to be sure to have enough to eat. He had to be by himself so that no cow, horse or pig could steal his food. After he put on some weight I let him outside to roll in the dust, to gallop around the corral and kick up his heels. He was overjoyed with himself for feeling so well.

The first time he came trotting to me, braying breathlessly as he came, I felt that I was receiving a favor. Softly he put his muzzle into my hand. It was a pink muzzle with tiny freckles on it. I tickled his nostrils with my fingers, stroked his wonderful ears. When I moved away he followed me.

Domingo made me happy because he was one creature that I could help. For the trapped coyotes, the wounded deer, there was nothing to be done. For Domingo there was much.

The burro was offered friendship by the pigs but this he did not like. He did not know pig language. A pig makes many different sounds, one of which asks for friendship. But Domingo did not know this so he gave a half snort, half squeal, turned quickly, kicked up his heels and ran for his life whenever Little Brother, Hamlet or Wallace wanted to be nice to him.

One evening as I carried water to a cow and her calf, Domingo followed me, got ahead, backed toward me in a way that might be thought threatening. But that was because I had taught him what I teach every colt. Long ago I discovered that colts like to be scratched around the base of their tails, between their hind legs. Once they get used to this, they won't kick at people. As I carried the buckets of water, my progress was impeded by the rear end of Domingo.

After I got the cow watered, Domingo came cavorting at me, seeming ready to stomp me down. As he reached me, he stood on his hind legs as if about to embrace me with his fore ones, then dropped his front hoofs neatly in front of my feet. He seized my sleeve and started leading me around. This I knew was bad training for him but I thought it entertaining and endearing. He who had been unloved and unfed for so long needed all the fun he could have.

Every day from his corral he watched the horses and they watched him. Sometimes, feeling lonely, he brayed at them. The only one who didn't like his bray was the stallion, Don Roscoe. When he heard Domingo he put back his ears and ran.

The months went by and it was almost spring. Domingo, as if he felt the surge and growth of everything on earth, raced around his limited quarters and brayed to all the horses he saw.

It was time to turn him free. One springlike morning I put him in the small meadow between barn and house and I let my mare Rosalys, who was usually sensible, in with him. Rosalys took one look at Domingo, whom she had seen countless times in his corral, and ran from him wildly. He stood and calmly stared at her, seeming to concentrate with both ears and eyes. Rosalys ran to the nearest fence, tried to leap it, didn't quite make it, but tore some of it down and so got across. As soon as she quieted a bit I followed her and found her hurt not at all. But she kept looking at Domingo and snorting.

I introduced Domingo to the other horses, one by one. There were no further incidents. Attu and the burro ran and played together. Lynette decided that Domingo was either her colt or her little brother and fell into a state of mad protectiveness toward him. She tried to chase all others away and wanted him to cling by her side. I had expected trouble from old Tony, who is dramatic and possessive toward the mares, but he liked Domingo. Within an hour after their introduction he and Domingo were playing together, Tony biting at Domingo's ears, Domingo rearing to pretend to tear out Tony's throat. From his pasture Don Roscoe looked on in horror. Perhaps his mother had once told him that a burro can kill a stallion.

Before the end of that day spring seemed to be coming on so fast that I thought the time had arrived to let the horses graze in the barley fields over the hill. A tractor and disc had prepared the field during the rainy season, the seeds had been planted, and now the field was brightly green, the earth firm.

At sundown I opened the gate and let the horses gallop through—reds, bays, browns, one black. As I stood and watched them I thought about all the other horses I had known in my life. So many of them were gone forever, as though they had galloped into the sky.

And then I saw the burro, running in the stiff-legged, toylike way of burros—up over the hill where the sky was. It was almost as though he had disappeared too, with the rest of the gray mare's colts.

Judy Van der Veer has written many books for both adults and children, all of them set against the background of the Southern California hill country she knows and loves so well. Her ranch near the town of Ramona in San Diego County is home not only to her but to a large and exceedingly various animal population—horses, cattle, pigs, goats, birds, dogs, a burro and countless cats—many of whom have found their way into her stories. Miss Van der Veer was born in Pennsylvania, spent her childhood in San Diego and moved to the country while still in her teens. Her first book (for adults), *The River Pasture*, received wide critical acclaim and was followed by *Brown Hills*, *November Grass*, *A Few Happy Ones* and *My Valley In The Sky*. Then came her first junior novel, *Hold The Rein Free* (published by Golden Gate Junior Books in 1966), which met with a most enthusiastic response from a wide audience of young readers. *Higher Than The Arrow*, a story of a child growing up on an Indian reservation, appeared three years later in 1969 and has added to her growing popularity as a writer of distinguished books for young people.